The Tarot Toolbook
ISBN 978-0-9916780-0-6

White Buffalo Publishing

Third Edition - Print
Digital version is also available.

All rights reserved.
Copyright © 2011 Susheela Kundargi
This book may not be reproduced in whole or in part,
by mimeograph, or by any other means, without
express permission from the author.
For information: susheela.kundargi@gmail.com

The Tarot Toolbook

By
Susheela Kundargi

Preface

After many years of reading the tarot, (while studying symbolism, astrology, psychology, honing my intuition, and being an alternative therapist, artist, teacher & entrepreneur) I realized that I had never found a book that truly, concisely identified multiple meanings for every card.

As they say, "necessity is the mother of invention", after all. As the need arose, I decided to create this book so that the novice, the apprentice, or the expert, could easily use this book as a helpful tool.

I've designed the book in such a way that the descriptions for each card may be as lengthy as they are in other books, but I've broken down each card into the five distinct areas that people ask about most often.

In this way, it is more succinct while in a broader sense more detailed, as so many other interpretations focus solely on one aspect per card.

These definitions have come to me over two decades and have finally been compiled here. Hopefully, as a bonus, these definitions will also assist you in developing your own intuition. I encourage you to make notes in this book and elsewhere for future reference.

Enjoy!

Table of Contents:

Part 1 -
How to Read the Cards & Activate Your Intuition 6

Part 2 -
The Minor Arcana 13

Part 3 -
The Major Arcana 86

Part 4 -
The Card Layouts (Spreads) 119

Part 5 -
Combination Cards With Enhanced Meaning 132

Part I
How to
Read the Cards
& Activate Your Intuition

When first learning how to read the cards, the best thing to do is to find a deck that really stirs up the right emotions and sensations for you. The images, the colours, the symbols, all need to "speak" to you on a deeper level. I cannot emphasize this enough.

At the beginner level, it simply helps so that you can remember through a sense of knowing, rather than just memorizing. It's like studying for a test; when you actually know the information, versus just memorizing it. As you progress, it will greatly enhance your intuition if you can access your emotional response while interpreting. Subtle differences can arise when a certain card appears for one person, than for another.

Once you find a few decks that you really like, I would recommend using this book to narrow down your first purchase to just one deck. Randomly choose 5-10 cards and then read their meanings. See which cards visually cue your memory to remember the meanings described with this book. The more the artwork coincides with the meaning, the easier it will be for you, and the better your readings will be.

If you already own a deck of Tarot cards (or several, as the case may be) or if you are already somewhat familiar with the basic meanings of the cards, then use this book to delve into all 5 aspects of each card and see if the deck you currently use can trigger those descriptions for you.

Traditionally, the cards have had limited or more focused meanings. For example, one card may mean, "work troubles" and another, "lots of money". But what if both those cards were selected for a question like, "when will I find Mr. or Mrs. Right?" Does it mean you meet the person at work and it causes trouble, but then you receive lots of money so you feel compensated?

In this method, you can learn how the base meaning of the card can colour the different aspects of your reading. If you are focused on a reading for a particular subject, then you can use the specific aspects of 'mind', 'love', 'work', 'money', 'spiritual' or 'personified' in the appropriate position to give you a more defined interpretation for the placement of the cards as well as the subject of the reading.

The 'Mind' section interpretation can be looked at to understand someone's state of mind, what someone is thinking or possibly feeling, one's psychological or mental state, as well as ideas or concepts.

The 'Love' section interpretation is primarily used for questions pertaining to romantic love. In some cases it may help define other sorts of relationships, so it may be looked at when key relationships are questioned, as a secondary tool for further insight.

Use the 'Work' section when you want to look at anything pertaining to your current job, job searching, career path, people you work with, self-employment, business dealings, and even paperwork or contractual elements.

The 'Spiritual' aspect of the card pertains to not only what one might clearly define as spiritual, but also all things ethereal in nature. This would also include mysticism, the occult, higher learning/knowledge, religion (in its deeper sense, not the dogma aspect), the cosmic consciousness, and transcendental meanings.

If you're looking to the cards to describe a person, then the 'personified' section is particularly useful, as it goes beyond what court cards can tell you.

Now, this book does focus on certain set meanings for each area and for each card. However, if your intuition is limited or you don't plan to try to expand on it, that is perfectly fine. This book is designed to give you as much basic, yet concise information, that you should be duly satisfied with your divinations.

For those of you who wish to expand on your intuition using these interpretations as a guide, then this next bit is for you!

Definitely familiarize yourself with the contents of this book; rather than do readings at first, just randomly pull cards out and read their meanings. Try all the money aspects, then all the love aspects, or whichever aspect you'd like to focus on first. Maybe, first read all of one suit and one aspect. Whatever you do, it's best to learn in small portions. This will allow for more retention.

As mentioned earlier, the choice in card decks plays an important role as well. So spend the time to look at the image in relation to its meaning.

You will begin to notice affinities between cards, suits, and numbers. Then you can start doing a reading or two. It's normal if you are still unable to recall the details at this point; even with reading alone, you will begin to feel familiar and comfortable with the deck.

Your intuition has already begun to kick in. As you will begin to notice, you may be doing a reading on money, but depending on the position of certain cards, you will read other meanings. For instance, you may read the "mind" aspect for a card placed in the position of "state of mind" instead of, or in addition to the "money" aspect.

I typically don't recommend using reverse meanings as the result of flipping a card from the left or right rather than vertically, is too haphazard for my liking. This is where your intuition will come into play. Some people feel that having a reverse meaning allows for an instant doubling of possibilities that then compounds exponentially depending on position etc. But as your intuition improves, you will notice that tertiary meanings arise when cards are combined as well as placement and relative position.

How to develop or jump-start your intuition a little? Rather than strain for insight, just relax and let it flow to you. Allow images, words, songs, fragrances, and feelings to stir within you and express them as they come to you and move on. Notice physical sensations like your chest tightening, a headache, a bile-like taste, a stomach-ache, or alternatively, a warm, calm or peaceful feeling coming over you. These are all basic "feel good" or "feel bad" instincts and should not be ignored.

In the same way dream images appear and vaporize so do these conscious images. At first you may think you're just "making them up" but just say them aloud or write them down and see what comes to pass. These may very well be the clues you've been ignoring all along.

To prepare for a reading, calm yourself by closing your eyes and taking a few slow deep breaths in and out. Focus on relaxing all your muscles and release all tension in the body and ask for insight and opportunity with positive intentions so that your reading can be helpful to those concerned.

Upon inhalation, say to yourself in your mind, "inhale peace and tranquillity" or "inhale calm relaxation", or whatever is meaningful to you. When you exhale, say something like, "exhaling all stress and tension". Do this a few times until you feel that you are ready to start.

Then open your eyes and begin. Some people never let anyone else touch their cards, and for others, they insist upon it. You will have to decide what feels right to you.

A variety of spreads (layouts) are listed at the back of this book. Based on the type of question(s) you're attempting to answer, you will choose an appropriate spread.

If you or the querent is shuffling the cards, then for the first period of shuffling focus on returning the cards to neutral, then mentally ask your question as you continue shuffling. Place the deck facedown and cut it with the left hand once. Replace the bottom half of the deck onto the top half to make one full deck again. The card showing now at the bottom of the deck, is the cut card; it sort of flavours the feeling or general subject of the reading. Then from the top of the deck, choose cards in sequence to fill the positions within any given spread.

Another method for card selection is to spread all the cards of the deck face down on the table. Spread them around until their backs are all mostly exposed. Begin selecting cards at random. In a similar way, that is somewhat a combination of the two methods, you can shuffle, cut if desired but then spread the cards on the table in fan patterns on in a line, then randomly choose the number of necessary cards. Always keeping your focus upon the question at hand.

Part II
The Minor Arcana

The Suits of:

Swords, Disks, Cups, & Wands

& their meanings in terms of the mind, love, work, money, spirituality, and personified.

Suit of Swords

The Sword cards generally represent the ethereal quality of air and the intangible forms of thought and learning. They encompass all matters related to education, transference of knowledge, ideas, and simple or complex thought processes.

Swords are also symbolic of severing, slashing, stabbing, or staking in real life and so are they also in the Tarot. They are metallic and so are rigid yet flexible, heavy yet can be incredibly precise.

A great deal of the sword cards have a negative aura about them compared to cards of the other three suits.

Ace of Swords

Mind

When the Ace of Swords appears in a reading meant to uncover one's state of mind, it can signal that the questioner's mind is ready for new learning, to start an area of study, or has a bright idea. It is a positive card and is always interpreted with optimism and symbolizes clear thinking or fresh thought.

Love

In terms of love, the Ace of Swords means that the relationship is probably still in its early stages (surrounding cards would clarify whether this is the case or not) but it surely signifies that there is considerable analyzing going on with regards to the relationship itself. There is more thinking than feeling involved and that is not necessarily a bad thing. It simply means that either one or both parties may be slightly unsure and is looking for facts and keeping a mental note of events and behaviours so that a track record can be created for later comparison.

Work

A new phase of learning is coming into play with work. It may be supplementary training, provided by an employer, or the questioner plans to learn more in order to enhance their job awareness. It typically is not representative of learning or uncovering information about people at work.

Money

If you are hoping to increase cash flow, the Ace of Swords is usually a good sign especially if surrounding cards favour it. It can be a discussion about money that leads to a new way to increase earnings. It can also mean that your thoughts about money are clearer and more focused, uncluttered by negative influences of the past.

Spiritual

The Ace of Swords symbolizes the beginning of an intuitive phase, an epiphany, or enlightenment of some sort.

Personified

This card can represent someone who is full of ideas, cuts to the heart of the matter, or who can see straight through a problem.

Two of Swords

Mind

You are seeing only one angle of the situation; going through your actions with blinders on. It may be out of sheer stubbornness and self-righteousness or it may be necessary to stay focused. Only surrounding cards can clarify which is the case.

Love

In terms of love, one or both parties do not want to see what is really happening. They hold on to ideas they have in their head rather than brave reality. In this case, reality may be pleasant or not but the unwillingness to look is the true detriment of the situation.

Work

At work, you can look at this in two ways. In one way, you may have to shut out everyone and everything in order to stay on top of your duties or obligations. On the other hand, you or your colleagues, are being narrow-minded and are unwilling to modify change for the sake of improvement.

Money

When this card appears with regards to money, you are being miserly. This card alone is not indicative of whether or not it is necessary to be so.

Spiritual

Beware of this card in terms of spiritual matters, for you risk becoming fanatical in your approach. Step back and look at things from another perspective in order to gain greater insight.

Personified

Typically this card symbolizes a person who is focused, driven, unfailing, and committed. However, in a negative sense, they can be frugal to a fault, narrow-minded, or obsessive.

Three of Swords

Mind

You are plagued by sorrow. This can be brought about by a single unpleasant event or you may be depressed, full of angst and woe.

Love

This is one of the saddest cards in the deck. When in appears in love matters, it symbolized loss, separation, and generally a broken heart.

Work

There is a trying situation at work, where you find yourself at your wit's end, wondering how the situation can be turned around.

Money

If this card appears in terms of money, it can mean that you lose a significant amount of money, or that money you were counting on, never arrives. It can also mean acquiring "sad-money", i.e.: by way of inheritance etc.

Spiritual

You desperately ask for salvation, because your heart, as well as your higher self, aches for a deep love.

Personified

A depressed or seriously ill person.

Four of Swords

Mind

Whatever your state of mind, the four of swords signals that you need to rest, retreat, and do whatever is necessary to remove yourself from the situation. Nothing more can be accomplished until your brain, not to mention the body, has had a chance to recuperate. Contemplate without taking action. It's time for self-examination.

Love

In terms of love, depending on the placement of this card & surrounding cards, it could indicate a bed - spending time in a bed for pleasure, comfort, or recuperation. It can also suggest, the need to retreat from a relationship in order to uncover any hidden motives or at the very least, determine what is driving the relationship.

Work

When this sword appears in your reading, the best thing to do is stay silent and observe until the right moment. Hold your tongue, make no adjustments; just wait and see what happens. You can think about the future, even plan & prepare for it, but keep in mind: it's in the future when you will act, not now.

Money

Avoid spending money at this time, especially for speculation or pleasure. Not that anything devastating should arise, but the feeling that the money somehow vanishes, is prominent. It would be best to save right now.

Spiritual

You need to seek sanctuary of some kind. Retreat, take a vacation, pray, ask for guidance and stability.

Personified

The four of swords can represent a therapist of any sort or someone confined to a bed.

Five of Swords

Mind

You are not behaving with integrity at this time and your thoughts are highly questionable, not to mention your motives. Before you act, please reconsider what is right and do not do anything based on personal interest or obsession.

Love

One (or both parties) in the relationship is behaving in a questionable manner, focusing on self-interest alone, ill-gotten gains, manipulation, and mind-games. It has ceased to be a loving exchange and instead, the parties no longer care about each other's welfare or interests.

Work

There are many things going on that could make your work situation unpleasant at this time. Either you, or the people you work with, are involved with unethical business practices, and are creating an environment riddled with conflict. There may even be illegal or criminal activities taking place.

Money

The five of swords shows manipulation through money. Either the money gained was through illegal, criminal, or devious means, or simply that a complete lack of integrity was involved. If you are entering into a business deal, be very wary about someone asking for money for they are misrepresenting themselves or the situation.

Spiritual

You are in need of finding your way to the righteous path once again. You have completely lost your sense of morals and ethics, or have engaged in activities that lack integrity. Any apparent victory at this time, will soon dissolve into prolonged dissatisfaction, because the means justified the end without sufficient care to ensure that the action was the right thing to do for all involved.

Personified

This card represents a very dishonest person, who lacks integrity and reliability. In the best sense, this can be a person who has to look out for him or herself because nobody else will. But usually it's a person who is doing this for manipulative & selfish reasons alone.

Six of Swords

Mind

There is a renewed sense of optimism with the six of swords as you move out of the self-doubt, the despair, or the retreat. There is also a sense that things don't have to be so difficult, and you allow new ideas, people, and things, to flow to you or you to them.

Love

The effects of this card can be greatly enhanced by surrounding cards of a positive nature. The six signals moving to a happier place either physically or emotionally, letting go of rigid ideals or old habits.

Work

At work you may feel as if everything is changing, maybe for the better but you feel slightly uprooted and unsettled during this time. Your job may require you to do some travelling, take business trips, or change location. Movement with this card is generally favourable, but not exceedingly.

Money

Money is flowing with the six of swords but it's not growing yet. You can manage with what you have, and are rightly optimistic, but you may have to juggle for some time until things improve drastically. Hold tight, be patient, it will happen soon if you can stay the course.

Spiritual

You are on the road to recovery; things are improving as you come out of the fog. You may not be thrilled, but you are no longer depressed or confused. Things are opening up and you can finally feel it. You've past through the hardest part.

Personified

This card can represent a sea-traveller, or a facilitator.

Seven of Swords

Mind

Mentally, you are quite withdrawn, preferring the solitude of your own thoughts, uninterrupted by people with whom you are not yet prepared to deal. If you must interact with others you project a coldness that makes it almost impossible to be approached.

Love

You keep the other person at a distance (or the other way around) being unable to partake fully in a relationship and keeping things to yourself. It can signify that you or the other person is afraid to have to depend on anyone else, and at the same time making it very difficult to be loved, creating a cycle that results in self-sabotage unless the behaviour stops.

Work

You are shirking your responsibilities, procrastinating, and failing to do the minimum of what's expected of you. By creating an atmosphere of deception or secrecy, you may become accused of something that you had no part in. There may also be many things at work going on behind the scenes that are dishonourable and will affect you whether you know about them or not.

Money

Take care of your money and possessions at this time for the seven of swords indicates secrecy, thievery, and dealing with people who are not what they seem.

Spiritual

Although there is great strength to be had in doing things for yourself, being independent or self-sufficient, when

this card appears, you are spending too much time alone and it's not creating the most positive results.
Sometimes, relying on others allows them to learn to give love, while teaching yourself how to receive the love and abundance that you crave.

Personified

Often times this card symbolizes a spy, someone behind the scenes, a loner, or an investigator.

Eight of Swords

Mind

The eight of swords suggests that you are suffering from a victim's mentality and are not actually a physical victim in anyway. As hard as it is to accept, even if you have become a physical victim, it's your attitude that achors you there. Do not wait for a saviour, change your mind and you will change everything.

Love

You feel trapped in a situation that no longer suits you. You may be unable to enter into a new relationship or leave an old one. The worst part is that you can't foresee a way out.

Work

You have limited options right now, especially if you are trying to change jobs, careers, or an element of your current job. Your hands are tied with limited resources or budget.

Money

The eight of swords restricts your money flow right now. You will find it difficult to get your hands on money that is owed to you, things will go wrong with your banking or technology, and if you do have money at your disposal, the difficulty will lie in finding the right thing to purchase. All money transactions are strained regardless of the amount available.

Spiritual

You find yourself in a precarious position. With this card, you have all but given up hope and await salvation from an unknown source. Your higher self does not want this for you; you must seek clarity through guidance to put an end to your confusion and victimization.

Personified

The eight of swords represents a person who is unable to free themselves from bondage, victims.

Nine of Swords

Mind

You are plagued with anguishing thoughts of despair or frustration derived from the inability to see a way out. You are overwhelmed and feel guilty for not having done enough, having done the wrong thing, or missing an opportunity altogether.

Love

The nine of swords symbolizes the need to forgive yourself (or possibly someone else, but the focus of this sword is typically inward). You cannot get over a loss, an indiscretion, or a failure, and you beat yourself up over it repeatedly. There is a lot of guilt surrounding you, and it always seems rather unjustified with this card.

Work

At work you're going through a very anxious or tense period. Tempers are easily ignited and you feel burdened or overwhelmed by the circumstances.

Money

You will not listen to anyone right now when it comes to financial advice. You are unable to believe that there is any more you could have done or can do, short of waiting for a miracle to arrive. Until you learn to forgive yourself, and look to the future, you will drag yourself deeper (into debt).

Spiritual

The key lies in forgiveness. Guilt is a deadly thing to hold onto as well. You feel depressed, unimpressed with others, unable to see a new way, and punish yourself so that even if something good tried to come your way, you feel like you don't deserve it.

Personified

This sword symbolizes a melancholy person who is pessimistic and weepy.

Ten of Swords

Mind

You hit the lowest of lows. The good news is that the only way to go is up from here. Through prolonged suffering and anguish you're finally ready to let go. Surrender & forgiveness are just around the corner.

Love

You are a martyr in the relationship that you have sabotaged. There is no need to continue this any longer; all has been lost and now it's time to move on.

Work

You are at the bottom of the food chain at work or you have hit bottom emotionally. Either way, you lack any personal satisfaction as everything you do is fulfilling someone else's purpose. It leaves you empty and dissatisfied. However, you'd still rather complain about it, or feel like a victim than take any real action. You still feel like the solution is beyond your grasp.

Money

Every way you turn, someone requires you to pay money for something. You feel like you have no recourse and that you have to fulfil these supposed obligations.

Spiritual

If you actually choose to be a martyr, make sure your cause is a worthy one! Otherwise, your self-deprecating attitude is just a waste of energy.

Personified

The person represented by the ten of swords card is a martyr or a doormat.

Page of Swords

Mind

By using your intellect, you can solve the problems that plague you, with clarity and objectivity. So long as you dare to do it, fortune favours you.

Love

If you communicate with your partner in a clear manner without the need to be right, without holding on to your own opinion so tightly, you will reach a compromise you couldn't have foreseen.

Work

As long as you act with integrity and accept the responsibility that is yours, you will advance and the situation will get easier and smoother.

Money

Your financial situation has faced much adversity but now things are at the point of starting over and you welcome this period because you are ready to accept the peace and calm that comes with letting go.

Spiritual

You are suddenly more aware, more insightful, driven, and are able to see your way through. Your renewed faith and acceptance, added to your ability to take responsibility for yourself and no longer act like victim, allows you to feel spiritually energized.

Personified

This card can represent a guardian angel or spirit guide.

Knight of Swords

Mind

The mental traits of a person, represented by the Knight of Swords, are using intellect over intuition or emotions. Being sharp-witted, critical, or a critical thinker is also accented. Often, this analytical behaviour lacks any sort of warmth, and therefore can be misinterpreted as callus; it is less so in reality, but this knight's sword still cuts. Try not to always have the last word or to give unsolicited advice.

Love

If you are in love with this knight, be prepared to have all your ideas challenged as well as your behaviour, your attire, and your intelligence. If this knight is to be on your side, you must prove that your cause is not a foolish one, because if you embarrass this person, you will pay for it for the rest of your days.

Work

At work there is a very competitive, egocentric, or arrogant person with whom you have to deal on a regular basis. But on the positive side they are smart, charismatic, albeit somewhat unfeeling, but they are probably highly knowledgeable in their area of expertise. Unfortunately you have to hear about how wonderful they are, continuously.

Money

The knight of swords signifies that if you are receiving financial advice at this time it is probably sound. It shows you making very clean, safe (but not cautious) decisions when it comes to finances.

Spiritual

Beware to not get caught up in dogma. If you do, you are apt to lose sight of the truth or, the thing that attracted you to the philosophy in the first place. It's time to step back, check your ego at the door, and reflect on how small you are. Contemplate the two sides to every coin.

Personified

This person has a quick, sharp, silvery tongue. They command respect but you should step lightly around them and keep your distance, because if you get too close you can easily be cast away. It can also represent an air sign person (a Gemini, Libra, or Aquarius).

Queen of Swords

Mind

This intellectual Queen is very much in control of her emotions and signifies heightened mental capacity and having the ability to get to the heart of the matter through the head. It also represents wit, or having an edgy sense of humour.

Love

If you are in love with the Queen of swords then you much watch your back and make sure to not step out of line. Although in a negative sense she is cold and unsympathetic, she happens to be reliable, dependable, and precise. If this queen represents you, then take care to let people close to you know you appreciate them in ways that are meaningful to them.

Work

She is judgmental within reason, so be sure to cross all your "t"s and dot all your "i"s. It may seem that no matter how much attention you pay to minute details, you will still be corrected and your work improved upon. As a boss, you will never know as much as this queen and will forever be in her shadow, but if you are good enough she will always back you up. As an employee, she is an honest & dedicated worker.

Money

The Queen of swords is a favourable card to have with regards to money. Even though there are no windfalls, your money is secure, well managed, and every last penny accounted for. If you are awaiting payment or money from another source, you can expect that you will get exactly what you have asked for.

Spiritual

In spiritual terms, even with karmic laws, you cannot go through life tallying up your actions or deeds as you would a balance sheet. You cannot demand that a certain action requires a direct and equal reciprocal deed. If you are giving freely in the spirit of love, then you should expect nothing.

Personified

This queen can be a woman who is an air sign (a Gemini, Libra, or Aquarius). She could be given the title of "bitch" from time to time due to her cutting remarks, but at the same time she reliable & predictable. She may work within the legal system, be a therapist, or involved with regulatory systems.

King of Swords

Mind

This clear-thinking and analytical King is swift and airy, pleasant and open-minded. When this card shows up in your reading, you can expect that you have wit, charm, grace, and the fortitude to tackle any situation, as well as the mental acuity to solve complex problems.

Love

If you are in love with this King, you will find that what he lacks in romance he makes up for with wit, honesty, and ethics. He is dependable, forthright, articulate, and a pleasure to listen to. There is never a dull a conversation or awkward moment, unless you are insecure and feel that you are unable to keep up with this lofty King.

Work

If this character is your boss, he will always do right by you, offering wise counsel, generous bonuses (if warranted), and will have an ability to eloquently cut to the heart of any matter.

Money

If you are looking for money to fund a project, are applying for a grant, asking for a loan, etc, be very precise and clear without conjecture and you will receive exactly what you're worth.

Spiritual

The King of swords is concerned with karma, fairness, and equitable compensation. As long as you are not expecting it, or demanding that the universe owes you something – you are sure to get your good karma now.

Personified

This King can be an air sign man (a Gemini, Libra, or Aquarius). He is righteous, disciplined, wise, and impartial. He may be a lawyer, judge, or authority figure.

Suit of Disks

The disk cards generally represent material things, money, and the earth. All that is tangible, that can be earned, traded, built, grown, cultivated, or created in any way is represented by disks.

As disks are coins, there is obviously a strong connection to money (or gold) as well as inheritances or trusts. Usually the disk cards are positive in nature in varying degrees, and rarely have an outright negative aspect to them.

Often times, disks will be referred to as pentacles, which are a variation on a pentagram, a symbol of protection, and as such add to the positive nature of this suit.

Ace of Disks

Mind

When this card appears in your reading it is a welcome sign that your state of mind is operating from a well-grounded position. You know exactly what you're doing; you are not treading in unsure waters. You are informed, aware, and are setting things in motion with very tangible results ahead of you.

Love

In terms of love, you are being very practical. Certainly this is better than not using your head at all, but don't eliminate the romance altogether or you will turn your love into a mere friendship. Although starting out as friends, with clear heads and practical hearts is often a wise approach.

Work

You may be starting a new job, or even a new business at this time. Whatever it is, you are planting hearty seeds in very fertile soil and you can expect that your harvest will be very successful so long as you stay focused and well grounded.

Money

With the Ace of disks in a reading you will receive a sum of money that will allow you start a new venture or acquire property or investments. It is seed money and could even represent a signing bonus or something to that effect.

Spiritual

You are very stable spiritually and are in a very healthy state of mind. By connecting with the earth or spending time with nature, that grounding effect will increase even further.

Personified

A person symbolized by the ace of disks is someone who works with their hands, a hired hand, helper, or assistant.

Two of Disks

Mind

The two of disks has you in a light-hearted mood. You feel freer than you've felt in a long time, unhindered and unburdened. Mentally you feel balanced, energetic, you are laughing more than usual, and you adaptable and open to change.

Love

In terms of love, you may have to balance work and play. Neither all one nor the other will make for a stable relationship, so now is the time to temper folly with practicality, and refrain from making any far-reaching commitments until you've seen more (of this person or more people).

Work

Work is productive yet relaxed. You will find yourself multitasking and juggling but all is within your capabilities. Work is actually enjoyable!

Money

There is a cautionary note to this disk: there is just enough money to get by. An equal flow of coins in, as out. Stay on budget, and you will get through this period. A signal will alert you as to when this can be changed or shaken up. For now, the key is to not panic or have anxiety over the tight funds. Just be confident that it is only temporary.

Spiritual

Having the ability to laugh at yourself is a very liberating skill. Practice it often. There are things that you cannot foresee, that you cannot prevent, because one way or another you have to go through them. If you can find one speck of humour in the event, laugh, learn, and move on. Be resilient.

Personified

Usually this card represent a small group of people working together or who are connected through a common interest.

Three of Disks

Mind

Your mind is rather focused at the moment and very task-oriented. This is not so much in regards to large goals, as it is to daily tasks or rituals. Your mind is set on small immediate goals and tasks, which may or may not have anything to do with a bigger goal. Your main focus is to not be worried about other goals for the moment but to focus on getting them done and clear the way for more.

Love

The three of disks has more to do with relationships in general rather than love. Even if you are enquiring about love, this card addresses the relationship components rather than the aspect of love. You are working as a collective, perhaps not even a partnership, but could be connected through a group of friends, a club, or team. In some cases, it can mean wrapping up a relationship, tidying up the loose ends before moving on.

Work

You are working well as part of a team. This is a well-oiled machine, operating efficiently and staying on track. You know what you're doing and this is an opportunity to prove yourself to someone who matters.

Money

As with the two of disks, there is a slight restraint with the three, but you are moving ahead and gaining ground financially. You are experiencing a good stretch of time where you have stayed organized and balanced.

Spiritual

You feel good about yourself because you have exceeded your own expectations. You are relaxed and comfortable because you are learning how to work with others and feel confident in others' abilities to assist you. You finally know that you don't have to do everything on your own, and your heightened vibration allows you to attract even more like-minded people to your sphere.

Personified

This card represents a person who is a good worker. They have little interest in pursuing their own goals but are happy and effective being part of the collective.

Four of Disks

Mind

For whatever reason you feel that you need to control your environment. Typically this is not a bad thing but it can quickly escalate to the point where you find that you are grasping to hold onto what needs to flow. By restricting the exchange of energy, things become stagnant and all your controlling ceases to be effective.

Love

This is a very negative card to have in relation to love. It is the exact opposite of what love should be: free flowing, easy, experiential. You or the other person involved is clinging to ideals that disallow the other's feelings and needs, or simply mean you or they are clinging to the other. Being in charge for the sake of their own ego, or forcing situations and circumstances.

Work

Work may become monotonous in its regularity and regimes. There is nothing new, and although this is not exciting, it is at least constant.

Money

There is more than enough money to get by however the tendency is to be miserly, selfish, or restrictive with funds. Hoarding money, possessions, or even information and feeling the need to control every angle of the situation is also represented.

Spiritual

On a spiritual level you are stagnating because you refuse to entertain any new opportunities or other viewpoints. You are too caught up in dogma to see that you are standing in the way of your own enlightenment.

Personified

The four of disks represents a person who is stingy, overly controlling, or who suffers from obsessive disorders.

Five of Disks

Mind

You feel alone as if you don't fit into any sphere right now. You cannot relate to others because you feel that your lack of energy & enthusiasm would repel others further. People fall to the wayside and you do not have the interest or the capacity to engage them in any relationship or activity. You are focused on the lack.

Love

Even in the relationship realm money may be a factor because you are so overwhelmed with the burden of just getting by that there's virtually no energy left to enjoy or work on the relationship.

Work

If you are looking for work you may be facing lots of rejection. If you are employed then you may be witnessing cutbacks on all sides. You are feeling insecure or pessimistic and are surrounded by a lack of support. It is not a good idea to change jobs, unless you have no choice.

Money

At this moment you are experiencing great hardship. No matter where you turn, you have to deal with less and less. You are cutting corners as well as coupons and you feel frustrated, alone, and in despair. There is not enough money to get by and so you play out various strategies until you have to start liquidating assets.

Spiritual

The spiritual body is connected to the physical. If you do not take care of your health, you abuse your body, neglect your basic needs; you disrespect your higher self, your spiritual self, your divine self.

Personified

This card signifies someone who is impoverished in any sense of the word.

Six of Disks

Mind

All the sixes are generally happy cards and welcomed for the most part, in any reading. In this case, the six of disks represents that you are weighing the polarities of numerous issues. You will arrive at a positive conclusion soon because you are putting in the required effort to view things objectively for the required time. You are not overdoing it. Mentally, you are at ease and balanced.

Love

The caution here is to not calculate or keep account of the love you give or receive. Give freely, without being a doormat, with your eyes wide open, and good karma will come back to you. The universe is noting your deeds and kindness and karma will take care of itself.

Work

At work you can expect to receive exactly what you deserve. If you were promised something you will receive it, so long as you hold up your end of the bargain. You may have to learn or to teach something. There is much in the way of give and take, but all is relatively balanced, even if it is not so immediately apparent.

Money

Whatever amount of money you were expecting will be given. Any delay is practically insignificant. If you are offering an exchange, you will be restricted to the norm or status quo.

Spiritual

This is the card of reaping what you sow and if you have it paired with Justice and/or Judgment be very careful that you have conducted yourself righteously because karma is coming to give you exactly what you deserve.

Personified

The six of disks represents a person who is exacting yet balanced. Conversely it can be someone who has bi-polar disorder.

Seven of Disks

Mind

This disk allows your mind to relax a little in order to consider how to get to the next step. The situation has eased up enough for you to sit back and contemplate how to proceed rather than to have to act hastily.

Love

In terms of love, you are assessing the situation and viewing things from a practical angle rather than an emotional one. At the same time, you want to know where you stand and where the relationship is going from the other person's perspective as well.

Work

At work, things are improving although they are not yet stable. There are new angles to consider, arriving almost on a daily basis. You are able to see the results of past efforts finally beginning to bear fruit.

Money

In terms of your finances, things are getting easier. There is a reliable source of income that allows for some breathing room. You will receive money that was owed to you, receive investment income, or expected money of considerable quantity.

Spiritual

If you are facing a spiritual dilemma, this card signals that you are correct in taking the time to analyze the issue from various perspectives. It is time to take stock of the situation and use your head.

Personified

The person represented by this card is someone who is connected with money professionally or is someone who is level-headed and has a balanced view of money.

Eight of Disks

Mind

Your state of mind is prepared to focus on the details. You can meticulously look at things, dissect all the parts, spend countless hours doing so and feel very accomplished.

Love

This is not such a romantic card in terms of love. In fact, love may have to take a back burner to other more practical matters at the moment.

Work

You are working very hard to perfect your skill in whatever it is that you do. You may be an apprentice or are working with your hands, or you may learn new techniques to get you to the next level. Whatever it is that you're doing, you are very diligent in applying yourself.

Money

You are too absorbed in the tasks at hand to even notice whether you are getting paid or not. Look to other cards to see if money is present or not, because this eight is no indication one way or the other.

Spiritual

Great karmic reward will be yours because of the arduous manner in which you are applying yourself to advance in your chosen craft. These skills build character and integrity and they will be rewarded.

Personified

Generally, the eight of disks symbolizes a labourer or an apprentice.

Nine of Disks

Mind

This card shows you being focused and directed whether at work or at play - it doesn't represent having blinders on or being overly serious, but attentive enough to possess superior ability, skill, or tact. There may be a tendency to think that there is only one way of doing something, and not wanting to receive input or advice from others.

Love

In terms of love this card shows you at a point where you are stable, and due to material comfort, share in the mutual benefit with those you love. Your lifestyle has improved and is easier than before.

Work

There may be an increase in money – earnings, salary, or a promotion. It is not easy or free money, but it comes with decent effort and some sacrifice. At any rate, the sum is substantial and typically is not seen as a one-time event.

Money

If you are searching for money in order to afford something new, that sum arrives without strings. The amount is given for services already rendered.

Spiritual

In spiritual matters you seek solitude, not so much like the hermit but more for the purpose of learning and proving self-reliance.

Personified

This person, either male or female, is an achiever, and in addition could be a co-worker, a friend, even a relative. He/she is someone worth emulating if you want to learn how to be successful.

Ten of Disks

Mind

With this card there is a well-grounded confidence in what one can do and a pleasant predictability of what to expect that may stem from wisdom, experience, or tradition.

Love

The ten of disks refers more to a foundation of family and interconnectedness in love as a group. It is a welcome card in terms of love in the sense that it is stable, long term, familial, and traditional.

Work

At work this card portends that the job has permanence, and is probably already a well-established company or will have a long life. It is a secure job and probably a very likeable position despite a possible lack of excitement.

Money

This is certainly an excellent card in terms of money however it is not a risk-taker's card. This is a sign to stick with convention, focus on stability, the norm, and the results will be, or already are, secure.

Spiritual

In spiritual terms this card shows you feeling confident with the results of past efforts. You are less concerned with lofty ideals but more with practical, long-term solutions.

Personified

This card can represent "the establishment" as an entity as in a corporation or an estate. It could also represent the family as a whole or the hierarchy of a family, or even one's ancestry.

Page of Disks

Mind

The Page of Disks is a card that signifies that your mind is shifting to a more grounded state. It may be the need to reconnect with nature or it may a call to maturity where you stop daydreaming and focus on practical methods of attaining your dreams. It also allows you some breathing room where you should no longer suspect everyone of hidden motives but accept what you hear as truth until you have evidence to support the contrary.

Love

In love you are able to attract not one but many suitors. You may be a suitor yourself, with playful confidence, speaking the truth and going after what you want without being overzealous or aggressive.

Work

At work you now are required to pull up your socks; your integrity is being called upon and you are fully capable of meeting expectations easily, more than you might think. This card shows that you have everything you need to expand, to improve, and to increase your standings.

Money

There might be paperwork, documents, legal documents, contracts, registered mail etc. involved with money at this time. Take time to read it all carefully and in so doing you will be clear and confident.

Spiritual

The key here is to trust and to communicate with clarity. Do not be intentionally ambiguous; be open. That includes trusting in yourself as well as others and have faith that the universe is guiding you with the intentionality of love.

Personified

Usually a messenger, person in uniform, someone bearing news, or delivering papers, is represented by this card.

Knight of Disks

Mind

In the most positive sense, it stands for being practically minded. However, even when dealing with mundane matters, do them long enough and they can seem obsessive. This card can be a warning of extremes. Things that may seem like, or indeed are, good traits, qualities, or habits, can become negative when overdone, and can become thoughts of jealousy, dullness, etc.

Love

The Knight of Disks is a loyal lover. Although known for predictability, and planning, this love is deep & sincere.

Work

Organized, methodical work is represented by this knight and often working with money, whether your job involves working in a financial realm, or you have to do a lot of business with financial institutes, company finances, paperwork etc.

Money

This is not a risky situation as far as your money or assets are concerned. Everything is right on track, steady, stable, well managed & organized.

Spiritual

This card applies to the practical aspects of spiritual practice. If you take the time to apply a little ritual daily, your objective will be easily gained.

Personified

This is a loyal, trustworthy person. He can be a boss, a bank manager, stockbroker, or anyone you are in business with. Suffice it to say, he is generally a good person, dependable & reliable.

Queen of Disks

Mind

The mindset here is to encapsulate feminine energies in a practical way. It is to be helpful, peaceful, and serve, not as a servant but a provider.

Love

In terms of love, this is a fulfilling card to have appeared. It indicates what people always want on a deep level: to have all their needs met emotionally and to feel comforted and protected, in a rather passive way.

Work

You can master your environment with this card. It typically portends working around the home, cooking, gardening, general upkeep or improvement, but also special projects and making a house a home.

Money

There is a steady flow of money meant for practical matters, where all basic needs are easily met. It can also represent spending specifically for the home or for food, or having to spend for a feast.

Spiritual

You have the power to manifest with the feminine creative energy that is all around you in nature. If you are not near nature, this card would indicate that the time has come to reconnect in that way and bring those feelings into the home and to the family.

Personified

The person represented by this Queen is a strong determined, yet passive woman. She is loyal, steady, a good cook, helpful and providing. In the most negative sense, her passive nature may lead to playing the victim. It can also represent a woman born under an earth sign (Taurus, Virgo or Capricorn).

King of Disks

Mind

Having a clear ethical mindset. Being steady and certain, kind yet analytical, supportive yet inventive.

Love

This King captures the power of Mars without the aggression. It's a strong, determined, loyal, systematic approach, but covered with kindness and generosity.

Work

At work, everything runs smoothly. Relationships & dynamics within groups have a cooperative air. General success, nothing rocks the boat, sure & steady wins the race. Stability & loyalty are highlighted in a positive atmosphere.

Money

Philanthropy is indicated, generosity, sponsorship, and overall favourable aspects to any involvement with money. Following through with projects that were awaiting start-up capital, or the ability to devote some time to such projects.

Spiritual

Strength of character, a balanced state of mind, creating your own good luck, being optimistic, and having the ability to draw to you what you need are all possible with the King of Disks.

Personified

This is a person, who could be a natural leader (in a humble sense) or businessman, boss, philanthropist, sponsor, or other figurehead who is in a position to support those who work for him or those outside of his sphere who he chooses. It can also represent a man born under an earth sign (Taurus, Virgo or Capricorn).

Suit of Cups

The cup cards are often likened to chalices and specifically the Holy Grail. They are beautifully crafted, ornate vessels that carry water or wine and represent emotions, positive or negative.

Mostly connected all aspects of love and the flow of feelings we have towards others, they also express levels of creativity, sexuality, friendships, and familial or professional relationships.

Ace of Cups

Mind

With this card you have a renewed sense of knowing. It's not so much intellectual as it is feeling knowledge deep within. It may be vague, but it's very comforting.

Love

The Ace of Cups represents falling in love, or meeting someone you instantly like. It embodies those feelings associated with a new relationship; wanting to become intimate, getting closer to someone, both physically & emotionally. It may also indicate pregnancy.

Work

At work, you use your sense of empathy to get along with others and smooth tensions or get work done. You are able to forgive mistakes, rely on your gut feelings, and create a harmonious bubble within which to work happily & productively.

Money

Take care at this time not to spend money on anything but necessities, as this spending spree will merely be fuelled by emotions. Spending large amounts isn't indicated but more spending on useless things that may not interest you once this passes.

Spiritual

This card indicates the enhancement of extra-sensory powers, deeper connection to spirit and being more in-tune to the pulse of the world and the interconnectedness of all things.

Personified

The person represented by this card is either male or female who has an optimistic, innocent, but not naïve outlook. They are empathetic, loving, and helpful.

Two of Cups

Mind

It's time to merge your ideas within yourself as much as it's a time to do so with others. Try to explore your talents, ideas, and then seek out those with whom to share them.

Love

This is a very welcome card because it shows the two people involved, coming closer together in balance, reciprocating love, and forming a deeper bond. It can also indicate making a commitment to another, which is then reciprocated.

Work

At work you are in good company with supportive & genuine people or at least one other person with whom you really connect. Mutual understanding, support, a solid work ethic, and being able to work well together, or coming to an agreement are indicated.

Money

This card is less about money *per se* and more about sharing what one has, or being offered what others have to share. Again, if you are awaiting a sign that an agreement or reconciliation having to do with finances or material aspects has been reached, then this would be a very positive card in that regard.

Spiritual

In spiritual matters, the Two of Cups means being balanced, more harmonious, feeling deeper love for another, feeling more connected to your soul-mate or on the lookout for them and more likely to be in-tune with their vibration.

Personified

This card represents a partner, whether in business or love, someone integral to a team, or someone who holds the key to love and/or success.

Three of Cups

Mind

You feel like celebrating. It may stem from having accomplished something of significance, coming through difficulties with exuberance, or just the need to be out mingling and socializing.

Love

In love, this card shows you socializing, either with one person but out among others, possibly at a party, event, celebration, eating, drinking, singing, and dancing. It may also represent an engagement.

Work

Your work environment is very easy going with a genuine group of people who enjoy camaraderie and are helpful in creating a well-balanced team.

Money

This card would indicate that there is money available for you to go out and enjoy yourself!

Spiritual

You realize that much can be accomplished in a team of like-minded individuals. You feel connected to the collective consciousness, and are filled with love and enthusiasm.

Personified

This card represents not one, but a group of people who may already exist as a team of some sort.

Four of Cups

Mind

You are very self-absorbed when this card shows up. This is not always a bad thing, but while being this way, it is more difficult than usual to see the forest for the trees. While you are too busy looking inward, or thinking that everything is about you, you may be missing opportunities, or may ignore talents/skills that could help you.

Love

In terms of love, you have a hard time seeing another's point of view and are not taking their feelings into account. Everything is slanted from your skewed perspective, and you may be withholding your affection, or may be apt to calculating how much love is spent or received.

Work

At work you are bored, feeling unmotivated, and have become completely disinterested. Things may have become mundane to the point where you no longer see a chance for improvement or change.

Money

Your money situation has become stagnant due to your previous unwillingness to think things through. You seem focused on what's not there, what's not happening, and need to step out and try or learn something new.

Spiritual

You are looking inward, spending time meditating, re-evaluating and taking time to reflect and dream.

Personified

This person is self-absorbed and uninterested in others.

Five of Cups

Mind

This card represents a sad state of mind or sadness looming overhead. Intellectually, there is a sense of having missed an opportunity or not being able to perceive the light at the end of the tunnel.

Love

There is a longing for a relationship that could have been, or losing a partner in a break-up or to death, or grieving over the loss. There is an overwhelming feeling of sorrow and disappointment. Seeking counsel may be in order.

Work

Take care not to fall deeper into a rut. With this card there is an inclination to lose hope altogether. Keep in mind that there is always a choice.

Money

A great loss has been incurred; it may be more of a blow to your ego than financial but the material world is impacted nonetheless.

Spiritual

There is a heavy resistance to change and the inability to see that positive change is possible. There is a sense of defeat, even failure, for the soul. Questioning one's existence or connection to god, the universe or collective consciousness is also aspected.

Personified

The person represented by this card is someone who is very depressed and filled with regret and sorrow. It may be a temporary psychological condition, or a more permanent personality trait.

Six of Cups

Mind

Being filled with youthful optimism, like beginner's luck, not yet jaded, and having a pleasant outlook. You may also be looking to the past when you were still innocent and playful.

Love

This is a very positive card for your love life as it represents an easy, genuine, and innocent love. It is playful, reciprocating, nurturing, and safe. You are standing up for what is good and right and having a sense of all encompassing love as well as specific love.

Work

This is a card of good teamwork. Though the people you are interacting with may be juvenile, or younger than yourself, but they are fair, honest, and equitable. The team cares for its members and there is support and contentment within it.

Money

You may receive a gift, or even a gift of money. If there was a financial bind, a debt, or lawsuit, you are let off the hook.

Spiritual

You are open and free. You feel satisfied, reborn, relaxed, and pleased on a deep level. Your ideals are exalted but without self-righteousness.

Personified

This card can represent children in a general sense, your own children, or the idea of having children.

Seven of Cups

Mind

This card warns of overindulging in fantasies. Much creativity can be expressed with it but by the same token, you can easily lose your grasp on reality altogether. Fooling yourself.

Love

You can become caught up in the fantasy of the other person, the idea of love or lust, or physical excess. This is not a time to commit to anything because what you see isn't exactly what is there.

Work

You are probably daydreaming, having difficulty focusing, neglecting the more difficult or tedious duties, procrastinating, and generally not putting in the amount of care and effort that is required.

Money

Take care of your finances. This card indicates wasteful spending, not focusing on the priorities- be it bills, health, work or other obligations.

Spiritual

Sometimes this is a good card to have if you've been holding on to everything too tightly. Mess it up a little, overeat, drink, party, spend, be creative and frivolous but don't lose control altogether or for too long.

Personified

A creative, whimsical person, who marches to their own tune, not truly grounded in reality, and who tends to go round in circles rather than make progress.

Eight of Cups

Mind

Your state of mind is weary; you may have lost hope, or are waiting for something better to come along. Regardless, the old ways aren't satisfying, and you long for something to spice up your life.

Love

It may be that your current relationship is no longer working for you and you sense that the time to move on is approaching. You may be waiting and yearning for a relationship to come along or you may be pining for one that has passed.

Work

The work environment is no longer stimulating; the tasks are drab and you experience a lack of enthusiasm in almost everything you do. If you are planning to leave, start slowly, but make the change completely.

Money

You may have burned out, or your financial resources may have burned out. Either way, a change is in order otherwise you will only experience more burdens and more disappointment. It may involve the need to move or travel.

Spiritual

It is time to try something different. Whatever has been holding you back needs to be released. The old ways aren't serving you and the only thing holding you to them is a nostalgic sense of debt. Time to let go and be reborn. You may need to visit a mystical place, a foreign land, or reside in a new location.

Personified

This card can symbolize a questioning person, a traveller, someone who is looking for the answer, looking to belong, or someone who continually looks at what they don't have.

Nine of Cups

Mind

You feel proud, happy and pleased about yourself, your achievements, and your good fortune. Be careful not to be smug about it or risk losing some karma points. You can also risk not being able to modify or change aspects of what you've been blessed with if you gloat about it.

Love

You are enjoying yourself immensely. It is a time of sensual pleasure, romance, assertiveness, moving ahead with someone, feeling cocky, being out in public, going for a fancy dinner, and being surrounded by beauty and opulence.

Work

At work, you find yourself getting exactly what you wanted, asked for, or wished for. You may have landed the job you wanted, or received the promotion, or got the best office.

Money

The money you receive now is not just to pay bills. You have a flow of bonus cash that may continue indefinitely or may be a lump sum. You are now able to spend on luxury items, arts & leisure.

Spiritual

You achieve that which you desired. Your manifesting abilities have been proven. You feel connected to the world, its energy and life force.

Personified

This person is a kind, generous, but potentially a cocky, individual. He or she loves to entertain, provide, donate, or be a benefactor.

Ten of Cups

Mind

This card represents peace of mind; it goes beyond contentment. It's an all-encompassing sense of connectedness with one's home and family.

Love

This is the ultimate happy card for long-term love and joy with a partner who helps you create a family. The love of each other takes on a greater meaning when a home, children, pets are under the same roof.

Work

The company you work for may be a large corporation or a few independent workers. It feels like a good family, with all the comforts, support and stability. If you're looking to run your own business, then the same would be applicable to the work family you create.

Money

You are well cared for. Everything you want and need is here, and for a long time.

Spiritual

You feel truly blessed, even blissful. Love radiates from you and you make all those around you happier by your mere presence.

Personified

A delightful, supportive, good-natured, generous and lucky person.

Page of Cups

Mind

Your thoughts are filled with romance, love, and giggles.

Love

Be more loving, let bygones be bygones, say you're sorry or say hello for the first time. It is the right time to open up and show your feelings, become intimate, do something romantic. Or, it could mean someone may be initiating these things with you!

Work

At work, you may sense a growing feeling of connectedness, harshness is toned down, a little more care for co-workers is expressed, and people are responding in more productive ways with less animosity.

Money

This card tells you to trust your instincts right now when it comes to money. Seasoned views might not be applicable. Never risk more than you can lose.

Spiritual

Spiritually, this card shows you being a little feisty, and somewhat unpredictable. You're trying on expressing some new emotions, and you're still working out the kinks.

Personified

This card usually represents either a young person or an adult with childlike characteristics. They will need to play the part of someone younger than you for the purpose of what they need to receive. Conversely, you may be the Page of Cups to someone older, in order to get what you need emotionally or spiritually.

Knight of Cups

Mind

This is the bipolar mind and all that it entails. It is prone to extremes of all emotions, actions, concepts, and ideals. You can easily burn out or come to a grinding halt with all that your mind is doing right now.

Love

This is a very unpredictable love card as the emotions involved can go to extremes as can the behaviour. If you're looking for a short-lived romance that can be anything from sweet and sensual to possessive and passionate, then this card ensures you will not be bored. However there is a non-committal quality and if you're looking for a long-term relationship, something needs to change.

Work

There is an unstable air at work. Tempers may be flaring, situations may be rocky, but amidst all the uncertainty, there are many surprisingly good things happening that seem completely unconnected to anything else.

Money

This is not a time to risk anything when it comes to your finances.

Spiritual

It is usually considered a good thing to be able to see both sides of the coin, however, the grass isn't always green on the other side; it's greener on the side that gets more water.

Personified

This could be a loving, romantic partner, skilled, sensual, attentive, and imaginative but then they can also turn to their neurosis and be flighty, unpredictable, even volatile and noncommittal.

Queen of Cups

Mind

Your mind wants to share, nurture, connect, and show compassion for others. Your intellect combines with intuition and your heart as if there is no separating one from the other.

Love

This card indicates deep feelings of intimacy, passion, of receiving love and being open. It's like a motherly love, or the love of a perfect wife who can give freely and completely all in one moment with a never ending supply.

Work

If this card shows up for a work situation it usually means there is no judgment, no glass ceiling, nothing degrading or unjust to contend with. It can also be a boss or superior who has a motherly caring disposition.

Money

Have no worries when it comes to money right now. It is not the time to focus on that. Take heed and attend to personal issues, feel connected and show compassion. By giving, you will receive.

Spiritual

With this card you connect strongly with your intuition, or even to another, telepathically. You know what's going on without having to articulate it and your senses are heightened which allows you to help yourself and serve others better. You may experience premonitions, the ability to channel, or have prophetic dreams.

Personified

This card represents the perfect wife and mother, or a woman born under the sign of Pisces, Cancer or Scorpio.

King of Cups

Mind

Your mind is calm and just, like a righteous king sitting on his throne seeking the right answer, the diplomatic approach, and a tolerant, fair outcome.

Love

This card symbolizes a stable love life with someone who doesn't play games or mince words. It is true love, decent love, unconditional love, and one that is long lasting.

Work

This is a welcome card to receive if you have been having difficulty finding a productive yet friendly environment. The people you work with are intelligent yet humble, efficient yet helpful, dependable yet flexible.

Money

You are in charge of your money. If you are not capable of making wise decisions, make one wise decision: hire a good, trustworthy accountant or advisor. Regardless, you may cross paths with a good advisor whose advice you should heed.

Spiritual

Learn to be fair rather than right. Be inclusive rather than exclusive. Choose serenity over excitement.

Personified

This is the ultimate father figure. He can play with his kids, repair something that is broken, provide for his family, and offer wise advice, a firm handshake and an open door. He can also be a water sign man born under Pisces, Cancer or Scorpio.

Suit of Wands

Wands can be depicted as a branch or twig with a bud, leaves, or flowers, a magic wand with mystical inscriptions and gemstones, or even a staff or spear.

Wands embody the element of fire and its ancient energy including the sun and spirituality. It deals with the connection between the surreal and the mundane, or the spiritual and the practical.

A wand would usually represent what drives us, inspires us, or calls us to action. If learning is implied, it's not simply taking a class; it involves understanding a body of knowledge.

Ace of Wands

Mind

This card represents the ignition of creative forces of all kinds. Your mind is filled with ideas, invention, inspiration, daring, belief in yourself, and is a boost to your self-esteem.

Love

If you are in a relationship, this card breathes renewed vigour into it. It can also indicate having the assertiveness necessary to make the first move with someone new. It can also represent having faith that it will all work out in its own time and way. Now is not the time to worry, now is the time to go with the flow, happily and optimistically.

Work

This is a very positive turn of events if this cards shows up in a work reading because it shows that you are able to solve the problem, conceive of a better method, break past limitations, allowing your skills to unfold naturally.

Money

There is the fiery raw energy available to you to use to go out and get money, persuade someone to buy your product or service, to have faith in you, or to entrust you with going forward. Although it doesn't speak of the amount of money or material goods, it indicates that you have confidence to acquire it or to put a plan into action.

Spiritual

In spiritual terms, your creativity and inspiration connect you to your purpose and with the divine energy of the cosmos. You are filled with confidence, as you watch synchronistic events happen with greater frequency.

Personified

This person is an ego-booster, a motivational speaker, someone who inspires you, and who is always enthusiastic to try new things.

Two of Wands

Mind

You are operating with a strong sense of authority. No matter what your profession, you are commanding respect by seizing the day and doing what no one else will do or has done. You are charting a new course. Although you may be seeking attention to stand out in the crowd or looking for approval deep down, outwardly you appear unique, bold, and original.

Love

You are able to persuade another more than at other times, and you are taking bold action towards someone you admire. You're not being shy about speaking your mind and are definitely calling the shots when it comes to your love life.

Work

At work this card shows you in a take-charge position. You suddenly know exactly what to do and people are listening to you. This is your chance to set the wheels in motion and magnetize all that you desire.

Money

Everything goes your way right now in terms of money including increasing your winning odds at gambling.

Spiritual

This is the card of 'nothing ventured, nothing gained'. Most of what we can quantify is visible, but from where you are drawing this powerful energy is a truly spiritual connection, whether you are consciously aware of it or not.

Personified

This card represents the archetypes of the General, the Leader, the Chief, and the Warrior.

Three of Wands

Mind

This is a quieter version of the Two of Wands where you are still leading but you are more integrated within the group. You spend more time thinking, envisioning, developing longer range plans now that the wheels are in motion.

Love

You are trying to see the big picture, stepping back to get re-inspired. After some progress has been made, now is the time to re-evaluate and then move on to the next step or change directions entirely.

Work

This card shows you throwing caution to the wind and really going for it, whatever it is. Intuitively, only you know what to expect, despite what others might say. Regardless, they will back you up thanks to your track record.

Money

This is neither a time for changes to spending nor earning, but of planning.

Spiritual

You feel more than ever that you are on a quest. Your dreams are vivid; your insight is far-reaching.

Personified

The person symbolized by this card is someone who is like a representative of someone or something else. It could be a spokesperson, a sales agent, a branch manager etc.

Four of Wands

Mind

You are satisfied after trying to accomplish something or waiting for a period of time to pass. You feel lighter, energized and even excited. At the same time, you feel harmoniously congruent with your plans and have acquired some peace of mind over this.

Love

There may be a celebration of sorts, especially if surrounded by other reinforcing cards. You may have reached a milestone, an anniversary, expecting special news, taking a relationship to a new level, a new love, a first kiss or other special moments of that kind. You may also experience feelings of exhilaration or a pleasant surprise.

Work

At work you are now rewarded, appreciated, or acknowledged in ways that you had only hoped for previously. You feel a tremendous sense of relief, release, and freedom from restraint.

Money

Although this is a generally happy card with practically no negative interpretations, it still is not specific as to how much money you have, other than you are feeling a new sense of freedom, stability, ease of expression, the ability to enjoy new possibilities or opportunities, and actually having a solid foundation.

Spiritual

Spiritually you feel much lighter, more spontaneous and energetic. There is a sense of understanding the basics on a deeper level than before and you are able to combine wisdom with jubilation, without cynicism.

Personified

This card represents an enthusiastic, bubbly person who still manages to have their feet firmly planted on the ground while being light-hearted and spontaneous.

Five of Wands

Mind

This card signifies what could best be compared to having a paper cut on your finger on the day when you volunteered to squeeze lemons for your kid's school's lemonade stand and it also happens to be raining, and you're left in charge of 30 wet, cranky 8-year olds. Irritated, annoyed, and trying to keep a lid on it long enough to see the day's drudgery pass.

Love

You are bickering, not fighting. Everything irritates you and/or your partner. These are small squabbles, blocks or frustrations that quickly pass.

Work

There is a sense of competitiveness at work that is not so friendly. You can meet the challenge head-on, but there is also caution because possibly you or the others involved are not playing fairly. There may be a sense of provocation, trying to get a rise out of someone, having your mistakes publicly displayed, having to fight, or simply being caught up in the rat race.

Money

This card indicates many small annoyances. It could be that all your bills have come due at once or everything has broken and needs to be repaired or replaced at once, but whatever it is, now is not a good time to spend money unless you have to and anyone else should certainly avoid asking you for money right now!

Spiritual

You need to step back and seek solitude. This competitive, irritating environment is not conducive to enlightenment. Partaking in these games, only keeps you farther from yourself and your connection with others.

Personified

This person is someone who always needs to have one-up on someone else, if not *everyone* else. They are usually pessimistic and irritable. Anything you do can set them off.

Six of Wands

Mind

Although the six of wands is a very positive card, take care to not think too highly of yourself for what you have achieved, because although you took action, there is a certain amount of luck involved, for fate to have handed you this victory. Try to stay humble.

Love

Be careful not to let your arrogance take over. You don't need to show off to attract or keep this person, they are attracted to the real you, so don't blow it. You've won, now be gracious.

Work

You have emerged victorious after a time of difficulty and perseverance. You are exuding confidence yet beware not to gloat or be condescending.

Money

If you were waiting for money, even winning money, or hoping for earned or unearned gains, you get it all, and better than expected.

Spiritual

You have achieved success, now it is time to cherish that moment of manifestation internally and do good deeds for others. Nobody likes a sore winner!

Personified

The person represented by this card is a winner, someone successful, and able to manifest his or her desires. They may a professional, an expert, in any field.

Seven of Wands

Mind

This card shows you determined and assertive. This is not an easy case; you are challenged, possibly mentally as well as physically, but you are striking while the iron is hot to try to gain an advantage and fight for what you want.

Love

You may have to prove your love, stand up and take control of the situation, don't let complacency overtake you or the relationship and don't sit back waiting for something to happen or for a random solution to fall into your lap.

Work

You are being defiant, resistant, and assertive. You have to defend your position, stand up for what is right, and not allow yourself to be a doormat. It may be a question of salary, a union agreement, an ethical issue, or other aspect of your job that requires you to hold firm because you may be the only person looking out for you.

Money

After carefully considering all the facts available to you, take your best shot and go for whatever it is that you truly desire. It's worth fighting for if you know this is what it takes.

Spiritual

This card represents spiritual fortitude.

Personified

This card often indicates a person of integrity, a defence attorney, pro-bono lawyer, or someone who acts as an advocate on behalf of someone more vulnerable than him or herself.

Eight of Wands

Mind

Your mind is all a flutter but this isn't necessarily a bad thing. Lots of information is coming to you, crossing your path, or being offered for your perusal. A vast amount of this information is valuable to you but much of it is also superfluous.

Love

If you are in a relationship, especially a new one, you will notice things starting to move quickly as if being rushed along to get to the heart of it all. If you are in a longer-term relationship you may be travelling with your partner on many short, busy jaunts. If you are single then this card indicates a sudden appearance of possibly more than one new individual in your life. When it rains, it pours.

Work

There are many changes going on but they are positive. There is much to do and you find yourself running around at lightning speed to get it all done in a short period of time. You may feel like you're flying by the seat of your pants but you are accomplishing things. There is conclusion and resolution.

Money

You find the missing links, information or money itself. Suddenly everything has started to flow again.

Spiritual

On a spiritual level you may be a bit overwhelmed by the amount of information flooding your mind, as well as your intuition and dreams at this time.

Personified

This person is a bit of an opportunist in the sense that they go from thing to thing, place to place, and person to person, consuming all of it, digesting, and then purging what they don't need and keeping what furthers them on their path.

Nine of Wands

Mind

This is a protective card where you have to "hold the fort", which may be literal or figurative. You have to be prepared for all eventualities and this may make you appear somewhat paranoid.

Love

You are sticking with it despite your self-analysis or over-analysis especially when it comes to past mistakes. Stay firm, hold steady and you will come through the other side having weathered the storm, even if that storm is in your head.

Work

You may be expecting disaster and so you should prepare for one, however, this is more of a test than a definite outcome. Even if you are tired and fed up, this is no time to throw in the towel.

Money

This is not a time to spend frivolously and in fact you may have to go into your savings or liquidate some assets to carry you through or to advance. It is risky but this is a test of perseverance.

Spiritual

You need to show your stamina; this will only strengthen your character. You are protected from disaster, so long as you show up and carry through.

Personified

A strong, protective person of integrity and might.

Ten of Wands

Mind

Your mind, body, and soul are burdened. You have overextended yourself and now it's too late to say no; you may be in over your head.

Love

You do not feel like this is easy or fun. Whether it's your relationship or the lack of one, you just feel that it's too much to deal with at this time.

Work

You are overworked, under-paid, possibly under-appreciated and you are so caught up in the cycle that you can't even psych yourself up to jump off the treadmill. Watch out for burnout.

Money

You are burdened with debt and lack of progress.

Spiritual

If you don't learn to say no, you will never get out of this pattern. You take on too much, often due to your compassionate nature.

Personified

This is the type of person who does too much, complains about how much they do and how nobody appreciates them and then does some more - a martyr.

Page of Wands

Mind

All Pages are messengers of some sort, this one comes along like a muse to wake up your mind and inspire you creatively. It may not even be a person; it may be just an idea.

Love

You are encountering a spark, not necessarily a flame, but a person full of charisma and inspiration to push you forward in love or some other area. They may be your muse and what you see and how you feel may be illusory yet beneficial. Try to keep your feet on the ground and not let them get the better of you. Enjoy the free love, excitement, and pleasure for what it is.

Work

This card alerts you to move past your limits, for they are actually self-imposed. Jump into new tasks, start off in a new direction, and revamp the old, tired methods.

Money

If you focus on your goals, take action everyday, you will start generating the money you desire.

Spiritual

This card signifies that the creative spark is there to ignite your desires, so turn your dreams into reality because you have the means.

Personified

This person is a muse. It's not that they don't care about you, but they are basic, instinctual, and embody certain skills that you may fall in love with.

Knight of Wands

Mind

Your mind has trouble right now sticking to any one thing. You flutter from thought to thought, restless and perhaps foolhardy.

Love

This is not the person who can be there for you long-term. There is something unattainable, ethereal, and elusive about this knight. You can experience fun, excitement, passion, and lust with this individual but not deep love. They are running - running from or running to, or just running around. They may present themselves as cocky and self-assured but that's just so you don't have to see the real vulnerable side, and if you try to, they will disappear faster than they appeared.

Work

Your work atmosphere is very unsettled; everything is up in the air and the plan changes daily. It may be time to change jobs, while you still have a handle on things.

Money

Whatever you are being offered with regards to money, when this card appears, is very risky.

Spiritual

Try to find balance when you see this card. You may be swayed in many directions, and this may be fine for a short period of time, but if you don't impose a limit on yourself or your time, you may find yourself devastated.

Personified

This is a stylish, sexy, suave person who knows exactly what to say to sweep you off your feet. Although they are not insincere, they move with the wind, so do not get attached or attempt to get close, they won't submit.

Queen of Wands

Mind

This card shows you with an exuberant mind, with strong, extroverted ideas that you are courageously able to put forth to the world. Watch out for the off-chance that you could go overboard with this and become self-righteous, irritating or even tyrannical. Typically though, the feeling is more positive unless surrounded by negative cards. Expect to be able to achieve anything you put your mind towards.

Love

It's easy to fall in love with this Queen at first sight. She is sexy, fit, determined and full of charisma and charm. If you are this queen, then you must already be aware that you are never short on admirers who swoon over you at every turn.

Work

This is a strong determination card, where things are on your side so long as you take action. If you have to work with this person, you are guaranteed to get things done, but watch out for the fiery side of this queen.

Money

In a reading where you are looking to see how a money situation pans out, this card will alleviate your worries. Whatever was expected should come to pass. It's not usually falling short, not often does it give you more, but the overall feeling is to expect what is coming to you, or what has been promised. As long as you are doing your part, you will be pleased as far as money is concerned.

Spiritual

The exuberance of this queen goes beyond the physical and material world; it also affects your spiritual world. There is a sense that you are on the right path, allowing the flow of feminine, creative energy to guide you in practical terms, and allowing yourself to step out of your comfort zone with a smile on your face and courage in your heart.

Personified

This is a feisty queen, full of optimism, radiating health, a real go-getter. However, if you cross her, she can be downright mean! She may be a woman in a creative field or health profession.

King of Wands

Mind

This card shows you having a cocky attitude and bold spirit. It's less creative than the queen and more action or ideas oriented.

Love

Being in love with this king is a little tricky as he is rather elusive. This is not because he doesn't care, but he has so many things on the go, that you may never make his top-5 on the priority list. If you are the king of wands, then you may be in a phase of cyclical conquests.

Work

New projects, opportunities and ideas are represented here. You should be able to feel confident in any new role as you have a commanding presence for the tasks at hand. There is a great deal of potential and the road is very direct.

Money

Sound investing, big projects, leadership and strength are money elements of this wand. Your money serves you and you are in a position to make it work for you in ways you couldn't previously. Times of doubt or indecision are over.

Spiritual

You risk being arrogant with this card. Finish what you start before moving on to bigger and better things. Not everyone can keep up with you and as a king of creative strength; you also have the responsibility to those who follow you.

Personified

This is a charismatic man who may be a project leader, organizer, promoter, and renaissance type. He also may be overly confident, or excessive in his pursuits.

PRUDENCE

PARSON

WIT

COURTSHIP

Part III
The Major Arcana
The 22 Trump Cards:
From the Fool to the Universe

And their meanings in terms of the mind, love, work, money, spirituality, and personified.

There are 22 cards in the major arcana ranging from the Fool (zero) to the Universe (twenty-one). They also can be related to archetypes psychologically, philosophically, or spiritually.

If you have a reading with a dominant number of Trump cards, you may presume that it's heavier, deeper, or more profound than one with fewer or none. With regards to the aspect of time, when asked by the querent, one should expect the events to unfold in whatever one would consider as "now".

0 - The Fool

Mind

The fool is the first card in the deck and as such it is a cards of beginning. Not to be offended by the word fool, it means more ignorance and naiveté rather than stupid or foolish. It's almost a wildcard in the deck, and can be interpreted as either a positive welcoming sign or slightly more negative than ideal. Things can go in almost any direction from here.

Love

When examining a love relationship, this card indicates things are very new; the situation hasn't had time to develop yet and both parties are unaware what they think and feel as much as wonder what the other party thinks and feels. Although uncertain, it has an air of optimism.

Money

When examining one's financial position, this is not a stable card to have. Things are up in the air, uncertain, but neither good nor bad. Looking to buy or sell, the Fool card tells you to wait until a more reliable situation arrives.

Work

Not a good time to implement change in the workplace unless you really want to shake things up and let the pieces randomly fall where they may. Close your eyes, spin the wheel, and see where you land.

Spirit

The suggestion is to open your mind, a new hatchling, what do you see? Take away any preconceived notions and start anew. Experience everything from the beginning again as in a rebirth of sorts.

Personified

The fool represents a young, childish or naïve person. They may be inexperienced or foolhardy, but they may also possess a *joie de vivre* that others who are experienced or jaded, might have forgotten.

I - The Magician

The magician is a highly skilled character who has a knack for manifesting, an innate skill for things yet tried, and a generally positive nature.

Mind

The Magician represents your knowledge of the arcane, the unseen, or the unproven. Sometimes, you just know what you know but cannot explain how you know it. Somehow, you have the innate awareness of the mechanism without the ability to put the practical aspects into words.

Love

This indicates a new life, or a new cycle, with wisdom and willpower. It can also show manipulation rather than letting things flow, or a sense of trying to control a situation or person.

Work

Very positive, as an indicator that you control your own life, you have the self-esteem and aptitude to manage and succeed. You handle all situations with ease and wisdom.

Money

When inquiring about money matters, this card indicates that the power to manifest wealth comes from within you. This can be good and bad: knowing that only you are to blame for your circumstances, but also you have the total power to improve the situation.

Spiritual

Being spiritually or psychically in-tune. It is a time for you to spend delving into mystical realms, the occult or to meditate.

Personified

This card represents a very skilled person who can manipulate the situation for good or evil. In the best sense, it's someone who you don't need to coddle, but in the other extreme, this person can be very wilful and sly. You have to see the neighbouring cards to indicate whether they use their power positively or not.

II - The High Priestess

This is a card that indicates balance of some sort, as do all of the 2s in the minor arcana. In this case there is a balanced attitude, or balance of sides, or personal faculties in most cases, unless the surrounding cards are negative.

Mind

This card represents the feminine aspects of the mind, also involving intuition and creative forces.

Love

Typically this represents a woman, or someone who is sympathetic in nature, self-sufficient, intuitive and mysterious.

Work

May indicate a superior female employee or employer, who is understanding, intuitive and often acts as an arbitrator. It also can mean having more education, or reconciling opposites.

Money

With regards to money matters, the high priestess indicates that some good luck is involved, but also things are stable and favourable. The use of your intuition is correct.

Spiritual

There are many mysteries at work with this card behind the scenes. It is a time of spiritual messages, psychic enhancement and insight.

Personified

She is secretive, mysterious, and intuitive. However, she may also be playing both sides, or may be drawn to the darker side and be influenced by her passions or ruled by hidden influences.

III - The Empress

This card is similar to the High Priestess in that they are both feminine and very powerful. The Empress is more practical than mysterious, more reliable and obvious.

Mind

The Empress represents thinking of all things pertaining to "woman" including the woman's role, the woman's attributes, thinking of women specifically or generally, influential women, seeking role models, or wanting to be adored or admired as a woman.

Love

In a man's reading, she represents the ideal woman. In a woman's reading it represents being strong and still feminine. It can also indicate fertility and motherhood.

Work

Good omens are around you at work even though there is much to do; you are capable because this is a card of productivity, ingenuity, and authority. You can take the initiative and your efforts will be well received.

Money

This is a very favourable card when inquiring about money. Good luck is on your side, and you have skill, knowledge and leverage within your scope. It also embodies strength and creativity with a warmth & kindness about it.

Spiritual

This card represents feminine, creative and inspiring thoughts. Also there are feelings of the big picture, motherhood roles, and creativity on a grand scale.

Personified

She can be a mother, a matriarch, grandmother, a pregnant woman, or a woman delicately yet powerfully in command.

IV - The Emperor

The Emperor is the masculine ruler, representing governance, duties, exalted positions, strictness, large projects, and big plans. It represents the intellect, as well as might, and most certainly, importance.

Mind

You are following the rules, guidelines, using logic and reason. You are not wavering from the course, not letting feelings, thoughts, or events steer you off course.

Love

It is difficult to run wild with this fellow but he is reliable, dutiful, and will commit to the end. Not to say that he doesn't have a pleasant side but it may take awhile to get to know him as everything is regulated, accounted for, and categorized.

Work

This card usually represents someone in an authority position but if it's regarding your work in general be sure to tie up any loose ends, take control of all aspects under your jurisdiction, and triple check your balances. Be careful to not over burden those around you, though, because they most probably can't and don't need to see things your way. In the most positive sense, you can provide a great example of how to be efficient and most effective.

Money

Your money is controlled or you are controlling it. There is restriction involved, and may also involve legal matters, forms, or paperwork. It doesn't mean that there is limited funds however, quite the opposite.

Spiritual

You cannot make an exact regimen of everything, although you may try. Some aspects of your life need to be freer flowing. If you regulate every aspect of your life you will become unhappy and unable to realize why. Loosen up, a little, even if it's just in your thoughts or meditations.

Personified

He is the father, or grandfather archetype or some other patriarch with commanding authority or judgment. He is not unfriendly, but order & efficiency are more in keeping with his tune.

V - The Hierophant

This card represents higher aspects of life on an interconnected level, and hierarchal sense. Universities, corporations, religions, communities can all be represented, and also spiritual/cosmic hierarchies.

Mind

To have this card representing your state of mind, you are interested in knowledge, possibly even esoteric or arcane knowledge. You find yourself drifting away to something new or just out of reach while still conforming to the ideals of your group.

Love

This is a very lofty, loyal, and devoted union. It's not typical, but what most wish for. There is a deep understanding between you that may never be able to be communicated verbally. It doesn't matter though, because others can see it, feel it and are inspired by it.

Work

When this card shows up, you are definitely not alone. You are working either for a large corporation, organization, institution, or part of a team. You will have to look to surrounding cards to indicate whether this is a productive and beneficial circumstance or not. Just being part of this group doesn't infer anything else, one way, or the other. It may be supportive, creative, and influential or it may be stifling and antiquated.

Money

With regards to money, you are definitely dealing with large sums, but it may not necessarily be your own. You may oversee projects or be part of a large fund, where great amounts of money are involved without you ever directly having it. By the same token, depending on surrounding cards, if monetary gains are aspected, this card would symbolize some degree of luck or inheritance.

Spiritual

This is also a deeply spiritual card. You may join a group involved in religious studies, esoteric teachings, yoga, or meditation, or even seeking out a mentor, teacher, or cleric for guidance. Typically, it means that you are not only trying to find yourself but find out how and where do you fit in.

Personified

This individual could be the head of a corporation, school, religious community, or a professional, including a doctor, lawyer, judge etc.

VI - The Lovers

It may seem self-explanatory, but the Lovers card not only refers to romantic love but also friendships, partnerships, dualities, and trios. Enhanced meanings when paired with 2s, 3s, or multiples in the same reading, especially when placed adjacent. Decisions, choices, and values are also aspected.

Mind

You may be preoccupied with sexual thoughts, fantasies, empathy, sympathy and physical closeness. It may get to the point of extreme frustration or high anxiety but overall, it stays on the forefront of your mind. A choice often has to be made; frequently a question of ethics or values comes into play.

Love

You may be in love, or someone is in love with you; in fact, there may be something in the air where everyone seems interesting or interested suddenly. This card doesn't always mean real love, but those first feelings towards what could turn out to be love - lust, attraction, and sex are what it's all about right now. There may be too many choices or options, but clarity will be more apparent with the help of other cards especially the 2 of Cups, 9 & 10 of Cups, which would mean deep love & long-lasting partnership.

Work

Having nothing to do with romantic love, in terms of work, this can represent a partnership, making good ethical decisions, being open-minded, and being supportive and cooperative. It can also mean loving what you do, what you're working on, your contribution to the project or the world.

Money

This card infers that money may or may not be around, but you have to focus on the team, the couple, and the partner if you want money to improve. It is not a selfish card, but a sharing one. Tithing may be something you want to start.

Spiritual

The other interesting aspect of this card is the idea that one plus one = three. You have a yin and yang component, but as they are joined, there is the union itself that creates the third element. Spiritually, you may wish to seek out creating that, not only in romantic situations but being fuelled by love to create something.

Personified

This card could represent a couple, a duo, a team, a partnership, the parents, or lovers.

VII - The Chariot

The chariot comes from the days of the gladiator and although you can have strength, force, and willpower on your side, you are also at the whim of fate, the will of your horse and the stamina of your competition. Do what you can and what you must, then hold your breath until the finish line.

Mind

With this card you have the mental stamina to move forward and see it through. Now is the time to be egocentric and focused to the end. Have faith in yourself.

Love

You will have to be assertive if you want to create a positive situation here or even a situation at all! Without being too cocky, you have to make a move or else sit back and let the chariot take you wherever it wants. You may not overly enjoy the ride or where you end up!

Work

This is a positive card in terms of work especially if you are expecting a raise, a promotion, another form of acknowledgement or accolade.

Money

If you have other positive money cards in your reading you can expect to be taken swiftly to your money or have it arrive swiftly at your doorstep. If you have other indicators of slow money, or money troubles, then expect that there is nothing you can do to speed things up, or slow it down for that matter.

Spiritual

There is something to be said for using your will to attain something but in spiritual terms, we are always trying to free ourselves from the bonds of the ego. However, the human experience greatly involves the ego; as our experience on earth is a matter of our own egocentric perspective. Therefore, you must learn how to balance the ego-driven and fate-driven aspects of yourself.

Personified

Often, the person depicted by the chariot is a professional athlete, celebrity or performer.

VIII - Strength

Unlike the Chariot that is all about drive and force, this card depicts the type of strength that you sense from a large tree, several hundred years old. It has deep roots, mighty branches, towering height, immeasurable weight, but it is quiet, immoveable, and alive.

Mind

With the appearance of this card, you are patiently sitting still listening and gathering strength without losing control, staying focused and determined. You are courageous, and forgiving with the ability to guide as well as persuade.

Love

This card represents a strong union. If the union is suffering, then use your inner strength to regain composure, listen, and be supportive. It is not time to lose your cool. Don't be too forward or assertive, but quiet and reliable.

Work

You are a solid foundation, beneficial to the group or the work itself. Your ethics, determination, and patience are paying off.

Money

Any investment, expected sum, or salary is stable, reliable, even, fair and may be increasing (depending on surrounding cards) but it is certainly auspicious at best or steady at worst.

Spiritual

The spiritual lesson here is to learn about forgiveness, tolerance, kindness, and compassion; how to be quiet and still so you can really listen to someone else, or your higher self.

Personified

This is a steady, reliable person, who is objective and trustworthy. You can be yourself around them; they can tolerate almost anything, but don't ask them to do anything unjust or illegal.

IX - The Hermit

This card is another nine and as with all the nines in the minor arcana, some level of completion transpires. It involves introspection, personal quests, solitude, attention seeking moves towards devotion and soul searching.

Mind

Mentally, you may feel burnt out and require time alone. The answers you seek are not in the outer world, the noisy, chaotic world, but inside, which you can only access when still and silent for longer periods of time. It may mean physically leaving your location for a period of time, or symbolically retreating or withdrawing.

There is a feeling of needing something but not being able to put your finger on it.

Love

This is typically not a Love-card, but if paired with other cards that would typically denote love, relationships, sex, or attraction, then this card would indicate more devotion to any or more of those things. However, in the absence of those types of cards, The Hermit suggests, withdrawing from all distractions, including relationships. This is not running away from problems, but rather seeking solitude to find solutions in order to return to the world refreshed.

Work

At work you are either seeking guidance, a mentor or you are such a person sought by others. You are also quiet or contemplative at work and are keeping to yourself.

Money

This is not a time of money - regardless of whether you have it or not, the focus at this moment is on other non-material things. It's not a long period of time, but while the Hermit passes through your life, your understanding is what's emphasized now. If you are really questioning your financial situation or a deal, then it's clearly time to thoroughly think things over. Don't be hasty.

Spiritual

This is a very welcome card, because you have the need, the desire, the drive, the devotion, and the time to follow more spiritual pursuits at this time and you can be relatively certain that you will indeed find the answers you seek.

Personified

As a person, the Hermit is often depicted as a recluse, Diogenes, or an old man. Although this is true to some extent in real life, it is more often symbolic of a guru, a shaman, a wise person who counsels, or a mentor. In some cases, it's receiving wise advice, information or a secret from an unlikely source/person.

X - The Wheel of Fortune

This card, is generally a positive one, and indicates that fate is playing a large role in the issue at hand. Imagine a wheel being spun by the Greek fates, and although this may feel very unpredictable and random, the fates can be influenced to favour you.

Mind

You are at a crossroads, but less in the sense that you have to make a decision as to where to go, but more in the sense that fate will indicate which direction to follow to fulfil your destiny. You may also be feeling lucky, or luckier than usual. Synchronicity, serendipity are highlighted.

Love

You're ready to take a chance, perhaps step out of your comfort zone. You may feel like you are floating along having been suddenly swept up in a new direction with a new love or new angle to an old relationship. You may also be gaining a broader understanding as to how everything is connected or what part you are playing in the union or in different unions being more aware of cyclical behaviour.

Work

This is a card of opportunity. If it happens to be paired with The Universe, or the Star, then you should be faced with an opportunity of a lifetime. Generally speaking this is a fortunate card unless you have been getting away with something for too long, which would indicate your luck is about to run out, otherwise, something you have been waiting and hoping for, is finally about to happen.

Money

In terms of money owed to you, expect a win. If you are gambling, you may not receive the largest jackpot, but typically it means you are favoured. If you have been experiencing money troubles, then the wheel is about to swing to your advantage. If everything has been going smoothly, beware of any troubling cards that are adjacent to the wheel, as they may foretell of the downside of fate.

Spiritual

Everything has its season, and during this time you are more aware of the cyclical nature of your existence. You also may be creating your own luck, using the law of attraction, or witnessing/experiencing a miracle. You can also suddenly feel like you are not the driver at the wheel of your destiny, or suddenly like you are!

Personified

This is either a lucky person, or person who works with gamblers in some sense, or who is a gambler himself.

XI - Justice

Justice is a balancing card, just as she stands there blindfolded holding the scales. It all settles or resolves itself with karma satisfied even if you are not.

Mind

You are seeking justice, perhaps fighting for the underdog, or you may be the underdog. You take it upon yourself to be responsible even if the issue doesn't concern you directly. In fact, at this time, you may be obsessed with fairness, equality, or justice.

Love

This is the time to either be rewarded for good behaviour or punished for bad. Fair treatment is the result of whatever you have done previously. If you are waiting for someone to redeem him or herself, then now is the time for resolution.

Work

At work, a decision has to be made, either by you in terms of what to do next, or a decision will be made in regards to you. All elements are weighed and considered, and a series of steps are laid out. The outcome has to be accepted, because it is final.

Money

Watch for legal issues, paperwork, taxes, estates, rules, regulations, trusts, bills, and payments. Look at everything carefully, seek expert advice, and then proceed. If you do everything with the highest ethics, then you will mitigate or possibly eliminate problems.

Spiritual

This is the card of grand karma. Get ready to reap the rewards if you've been good, or face the negative consequences if you have intentionally done misdeeds.

Personified

This person is often a judge, a notary, a lawyer, a mediator, or someone in a position to deliver or enforce a judgment or decision of some kind.

XII - The Hanged Man

This is a card that visually may disturb you, as a man being hanged is not a pleasant image to behold. However, in a figurative sense, you may feel like you are hanging, albeit temporarily, not until the death; feeling like you are in limbo, putting things on hold, or being in a stalemate situation.

Mind

You are changing your mind at this time or possibly even giving up or simply surrendering. If you have been pushing in a certain direction, or yearning, now is the time to relinquish control and let it be or have it unfold, as it will.

Love

You are devoted to someone, or they are to you, and things have relaxed so that everything just "is" without pressure or expectation. There is a sense of living more in the moment and not getting trapped by suspicion or doubt. Depending on surrounding cards this can be enhanced to the point of bliss. If surrounding cards are negative, this card can indicate that the relationship is stuck.

Work

You can succeed at work or in your career by looking at things from a different perspective. Let go of the reigns, release the pressure, and surrender. Think of others by enabling them to succeed.

Money

This is not a good time to spend money, but don't hold on too tightly as you will lose. Experience the positive flow of money or start tithing even if you have very little to work with. Understand that you were born to be prosperous and change your mindset.

Spiritual

Become thoroughly devoted and practice detachment simultaneously. It's not easy, but you will catch glimmers of it as you tweak your technique and you will peek into the divine realm where you view lavish abundance. A sacrifice of some kind is often involved.

Personified

A devotee, a martyr, an archetype of a Buddha, a Messiah, or one who sacrifices, is often indicated.

XIII - Death

Most people fear this card, but it's unfounded, as Death in the tarot is the least daunting of any deaths. It's extremely rare that this card would indicate a real physical death, but it does usually denote a clear end to something prior to something beginning.

Mind

When death shows up in your state of mind, you can be sure that you've changed your mind, your thoughts, or your position on an issue, quite clearly and (relatively) permanently.

Love

Your relationship has taken a major turn and probably is ending (which can be seen in more detail by surrounding cards). A change has been made, maybe an ultimatum given, a line drawn in the sand. If surrounding cards are positive, then Death can be seen as 'good riddance to the past' as you move into a new, improved phase of the relationship or a new one.

Work

You are ending something as you start something new. One door closes as one opens. Both doors cannot be left open; a decision is necessary. You may feel unsure, but that change in inevitable, so stop procrastinating and pull off the bandage in one quick swipe.

Money

Get rid of whatever you don't need, what's lying around, even if you like it, it's time to clear it all out. Get down to the bare bones to make way for new things. Streamline or bundle your bills, payments, and make life easier and lighter. Stop waiting for something to happen, take action and watch how good things start flowing to you.

Spiritual

Death is an important phase but it's not a permanent state; it's a transitional period. Let things die: old ideas, attitudes, habits, beliefs, relationships, and anything that doesn't support your vision or path in the future.

Personified

This may be a person who actually works with death or the dying (undertakers, morticians, grief counsellors, mediums, people working with terminally ill patients etc).

XIV - Temperance

This card speaks of real balance and harmony on every level. It may sound boring to some people, but it's the middle ground, not mediocrity. Think of calmness, ease, and equilibrium.

Mind

To be in this mental state is extremely positive. You are centred, grounded, pleasant, showing restraint without restriction, nothing excessive, no feathers ruffled and no tension.

Love

There is an easy, laid-back feeling where it may not be exciting or exhilarating, but comfortable and cooperative. If you were looking to make a decision, an advance, or a move, now is not the time to rock the boat.

Work

There is an air of cooperation surrounding you at work. Either you contribute to others' projects or they do so to yours, but however it goes, it's the perfect combination that happens without over-thinking it.

Money

There are no money problems *per se*. However, if you have been experiencing a rough time financially, this card doesn't show improvement on its own. The good news is, it's also not getting any worse. If your financial situation is positive, then you can expect it to continue flowing as it has been.

Spiritual

This card signifies good health in all aspects. You have found balance mentally, physically, materially, and spiritually. This is not the time to isolate yourself, or unnecessarily surround yourself with people who fill up your social calendar; it's something in between.

Personified

The person represented by this card is that serene creature who appears to waltz through chaos without ever losing their cool.

XV - The Devil

This card represents things of a negative, base nature. Including coveting, indulging, abusing, neglecting, manipulating, etc.

Mind

You may be obsessed with getting something to the point of using corrupt means to acquire or achieve it. Also, this card can denote addictions, or other unhealthy states of mind.

Love

You may be involved in an unsatisfactory relationship where one of you or both are not operating with good intentions. If you are not with anyone, this card can signify that you are not in the right state of mind to attract a healthy relationship; you may feel unworthy, unlovable, or that there are just no options, now or ever.

Work

Beware of corruption, hunger for money & greed. This card can also denote being controlled, enslaved or abused. It could also represent that you have become the very person doing these things.

Money

This card shows that you could be exploiting someone or you are the victim of such exploitation. It also shows excessive emphasis on material gain and losing sight of those in need.

Spiritual

This card indicates that there is an overwhelming negative or evil influence around you. You need to focus, on the positive, no matter how bleak things look or feel. If you feel like everything is just fine around you at this time, take heed and protect yourself against psychic attack, and keep your wits about you when dealing with others; keep safe.

Personified

This card represents a negative person, or someone affected by negative influences. They may be just a mean, angry, jealous, spiteful, or ignorant person, or someone who has let their obsession or addiction get the better of them, a thief, or someone who has hit rock bottom.

XVI - The Tower

This card usually depicts some catastrophe, but like death, it's not permanent. Even positive changes, that are very abrupt and that turn your whole world upside-down, may be described by the Tower.

Mind

You suddenly get it! This card symbolizes your "eureka" moment where you can solve the problem; you have the answer, discovered the formula, see through the lies, found what was lost, or looked in the right place.

Love

This is typically not a positive card in terms of love, unless the surrounding cards are all positive. This card will usually denote arguments, outbursts, having a crisis, having your plans backfire, and what feels catastrophic.

Work

At work, you should do your best to focus and stay quiet as chaos erupts all around you. Many changes are happening and you will feel unsettled until this tower passes through.

Money

In terms of money, this could be positive in the sense that if you suddenly received, won, or inherited a large sum of money, it would completely shake up your world. However in the negative sense, it could mean having to spend in case of emergency or similar situation that requires an immediate, large outlay of funds.

Spiritual

This is a cleansing card in terms of spiritual progress. Sometimes you have to tear down everything in order to move forward or build anew. You may also receive a revelation, or suddenly feel very humble.

Personified

This person is a whirling ball of chaos.

XVII - The Star

This card represents optimism, tranquillity, and the light in the distance on which to focus.

Mind

Your state of mind improves with the sight of this card. It alerts you so that you awaken that dormant part of yourself that may have brought your entire being down. You feel motivated again and possibly ready for something new or just to pick-up where you left off.

Love

If you are in a relationship, you have renewed hope, or are taking it to a higher level. If you are not in a relationship, this can signal that you are finally sending out the right message to attract a positive partner or at the very least, someone fun and tolerable! You are ready to open your heart.

Work

Things are improving at work, although it's not perfect, you are aware that you are fortunate and that peace of mind is worth more than money in many cases. You may have that inner sense that success is actually possible.

Money

As for money, you are able to give without expectation of loss at this time, possibly even being very generous. Finances are improving and you no longer have the feeling of panic or desperation. If you weren't experiencing financial setbacks, this card can indicate that you are finally able to make your next financial advancement.

Spiritual

You are inspired in many ways. You may have a burst of creativity, have renewed faith or optimism, finding your centre, allowing love, or experiencing the answer.

Personified

As a person, this could be a celebrity, (a "star") or someone who exudes that glowing light.

XVIII - The Moon

The Moon is a moody, vague, shadowy card. It's difficult to know what's really going on despite having vivid or even prophetic dreams. It can also symbolize a woman's cycle, or a phase of the moon.

Mind

You may have a difficult time trusting your feelings or intuition right now. It's difficult to know if what crosses your mind is due to insight, ignorance, love, or paranoia. You may feel bewildered or even depressed.

Love

It's easy to become distracted with this card, especially if paired with other dreamy or vague cards. You may be confused, untrusting, sceptical, deluded, anxious, moody, or that your feelings and interpretations are suddenly skewed.

Work

This card represents work done at night, or fields involving secrets, intuition, psychology, the occult, mysteries, or uncovering what was hidden. If it pertains to your own work, you feel unsettled at best.

Money

If this card shows up in terms of money, now is certainly not the time to gamble, invest, or do anything outside of the routine. This is because you cannot trust what you see before you, what is presented or how things appear at this moment is not necessarily how they will be in the near future.

Spiritual

You may receive messages through your dreams or meditations, but they aren't exactly clear and so they are unlikely to provide you with much assistance in the present however still may prove to be prophetic.

Personified

It can represent a person who works in secrecy, or who is involved with uncovering what is hidden. It can also represent someone who is depressed, delusional, or who generally has his/her judgment clouded.

XIX - The Sun

How do we feel when the sun shines on us, especially after a period of rain or darkness? That warm, bright, healthy feeling is exactly what this card is about. Everything that the sun touches is improved.

Mind

You feel happy, blessed, enlightened or you may experience a huge burst of creativity, optimism, pleasure or appreciation and gratitude. This card represents a very positive and healthy state of mind; probably the best you can ask for, including having a sunny disposition.

Love

This card means that you are finally ready to give and receive completely and freely. You are radiating love and beauty, truth and greatness. Whoever you are with or may meet, the feeling surrounding the relationship is an exalted one.

Work

The time is here for expansion, accolades, accomplishments & rewards, because you know what you're worth. You know exactly where your capabilities and capacities lie, and others respect and admire you. You can take your place on the stage, and bask in the sunlight and the glory, because your hard work, experience, and attitude have finally paid off. Enjoy the good times.

Money

Especially if you have other positive money cards around, this card means that you are on top of things. Your money has arrived; you are rewarded or are just succeeding in every direction you turn.

Spiritual

You sense that everything is all right and that no matter what happens, you can move through it and survive. You reach a higher degree of awareness and insight. In fact, everything about you suddenly feels like it's been revamped, improved or has been revitalized in some way, even if unintentionally.

Personified

This card symbolizes a person with a sunny disposition, or someone with a tan or sunburn. It can also symbolize a person who breathes life into everything they touch or every room they enter.

XX - Judgment

The Judgment card is similar to Justice in the sense that you will reap what you sow, karmic effect, and there is no escaping it. You have to face the music at some point and the time is now. However, where the Judgment card goes a step further, it takes you to a place of forgiveness and rebirth in the cases where you may have done things that you later had to pay for. This is not just a card of clear-cutting justice but of resolution and reconciliation.

Mind

If you have this card as your state of mind, you have a sense of conviction, as well as absolution. Go ahead and take that step with courage so that you can move forward rather than allow yourself to be swallowed by guilt, regret, lack of forgiveness etc.

Love

This is the time to simply get over it! Whatever it is. You have been wavering for too long, or holding on, holding out, staying stuck in a low level pattern or position. You know what you should do; do it.

Work

With regards to your work, you may have to change something in order to keep going. The time is now for a decision to be made and you can always feel like if you choose 'A' then you will regret for not having chosen 'B' or vice versa. So it doesn't matter; make a fresh start and deal with the consequences. This is not to say you should act hastily; the opposite it true. But you cannot sit on the fence forever. It can also represent discovering your true purpose or vocation.

Money

Whatever money woes had befallen you are now over. You can come to terms with them, improve, make the necessary steps, and have a renewed sense that everything can begin to grow again.

Spiritual

Gratitude and forgiveness go a long way in achieving, attracting, and feeling happy. A great lesson is learned when you can forgive yourself or others who have harmed you or let you down. It's time to move on.

Personified

Someone who can give you absolution.

XXI - The Universe

This card brings you full circle from the Fool. You achieve everything and are open to a whole world of opportunity. If surrounded by completely disastrous cards, this is so powerful, that it weakens the negative force of all of them.

Mind

You feel fulfilled and accomplished having used the gifts you were born with. You have the sense that all is connected and that you are an integral part of it.

Love

Love is all around you!

Work

You are succeeding with your work, you are achieving what deeply satisfies you, and you feel that all your dreams are coming true.

Money

You have no money troubles when this card appears, so long as you continue to listen to your heart, all is provided for.

Spiritual

This card shows you reaching a deep level of understanding. It's so deep in fact, that it goes beyond words, or thoughts but it's in your cells & in your soul.

Personified

The Universe card represents a deity, a saint, an alien, a spirit guide, or other highly evolved being.

Part IV
Card Layouts
or Spreads
(as they're most commonly called)
From the
Quick and Basic
to the
Lengthy and Detailed

As mentioned in the beginning of this book, it is recommended that you prepare yourself mentally, and relax physically. The way in which you phrase your question is also important. Except for the One-Card Quickie method, try not to ask your questions in such a way that they would require a yes/no answer. In the same way we try to ask open-ended questions when having a conversation with someone, we ask them in card readings so that the cards can speak to us.

The One Card Quickie

Purpose

Use this spread when you want to cut to the chase, or if you need a yes/no answer, need to identify a person or their traits, want a simple answer, or need clarification without ambiguity.

Preparation

You can use the fan method or cut-card method (when you simply cut the deck and the facing card is the card you read).

Spread

This reading is hardly in a spread but you can continue to pull single cards and read them individually.

Interpretation

For yes/no questions, the stronger the positive or negative aspect, the more Yes, or more No your answer is. Be careful when asking questions, that they are not ambiguous.

Past, Present, Future

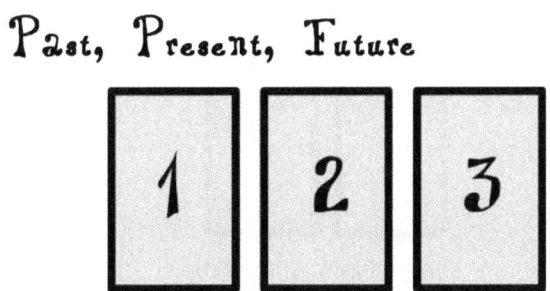

Purpose

This spread helps determine how something will unfold and to see where you are at in relation to it.

Spread

Lay the cards out from left to right.

Card 1: Past, Card 2: Present, & Card 3: Future.

Interpretation

The time frame from past to future is usually 6 weeks, at most, and the so-called present may be a period of 3 weeks altogether, encapsulating what we may typically think of as past & future. What we have to keep in mind with this spread is that each card represents a flavour or an influence that lasts for a certain period of time.

Pay extra close attention if all 3 cards of the same suit, same number, or all Trump cards.

Three Layers

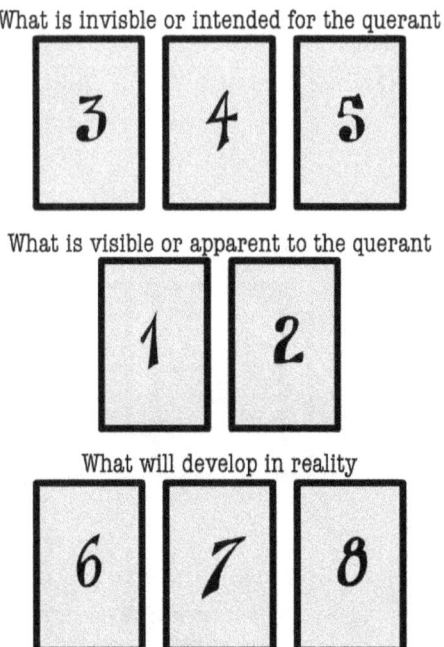

Purpose

Use this spread when looking for more depth after a reading like the Past, Present, and Future Spread. It can also elaborate on intentions, probabilities, feelings and thoughts in relation to an individual or a situation and contrasting that against the reality that may not be obvious.

Spread

The first two cards are laid out side by side and are read together. Then three cards are laid out above them and read together, and finally, three more are laid out below and are read together.

Interpretation

See diagram. Read each grouping of cards together.

The Celtic Cross

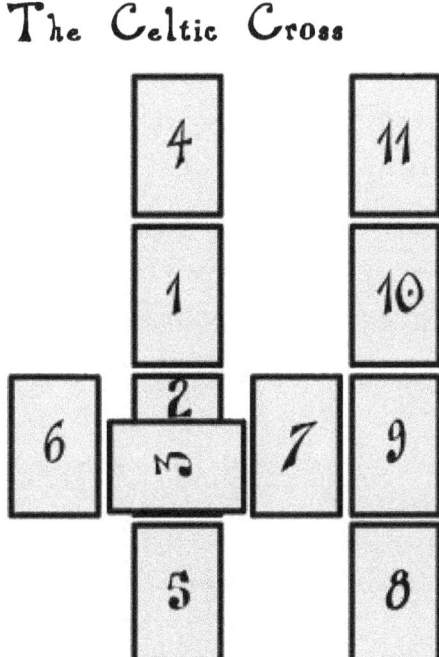

Purpose

This spread is probably the most popular one of all. It is a good choice for determining any subject, first with a synopsis of the subject, the current state of affairs, how we've arrived at this point and then a plausible course of action, influences, and outcome.

Spread

Card 1:   Querent's state of mind.

Card 2:   The Querent's present environment.

Card 3:   An obstacle or hurdle in the present, but if it's a positive card it can mean something that looks good but isn't, or something that remains elusive.

Card 4:   The crowning card; separate from the reading but in the ether.

Card 5:   A foundation of the situation.
Card 6:   The immediate past, soon to be released.
Card 7:   The immediate future, soon to appear.
Card 8:   The future environment.
Card 9:   The influence of friends & family (or colleagues, as the case may be).
Card 10:   What will happen just before the outcome; that which you may fear, of which you may need to let go, the crux.
Card 11:   The outcome!

The Celtic Cross Addition

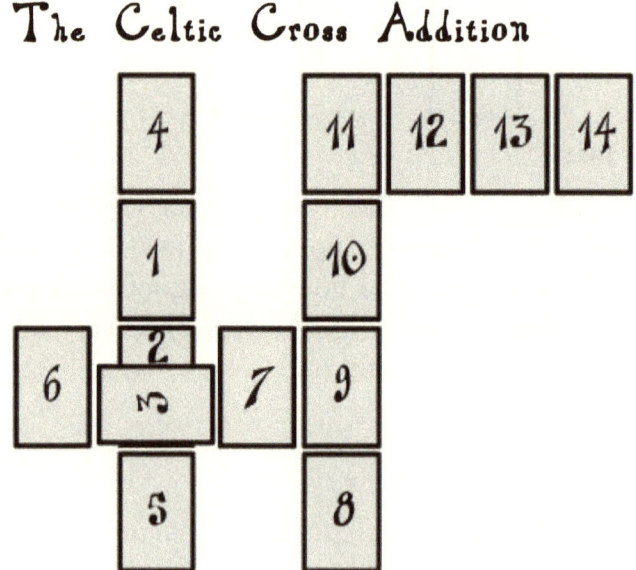

Purpose

If the outcome of the previous spread still leaves you hanging at the precipice of your query, then draw another 3 cards from the top of the same deck, without reshuffling or cutting.

Spread

Card 12: Gives you more information about the outcome card.

Card 13: A timing card (finally!) Read the number plus: Cups represents a measure of days, Wands are for weeks, Disks for Months, Trump cards all represent the present (ignore numbers), and swords mean that timing is still unknown.

Card 14: Tells you if the outcome is permanent. For example, if the card in position 11 is unsatisfactory or negative, and card no. 12 shows some movement or progress, and the final card is also positive then you could assume that the "outcome" was a result of the process of the preceding cards, but the final card is what holds more meaning. Conversely, if the outcome shows a positive card, and cards 12 & 14 are negative, then you could assume that the outcome is short-lived.

The Soul Mate Process

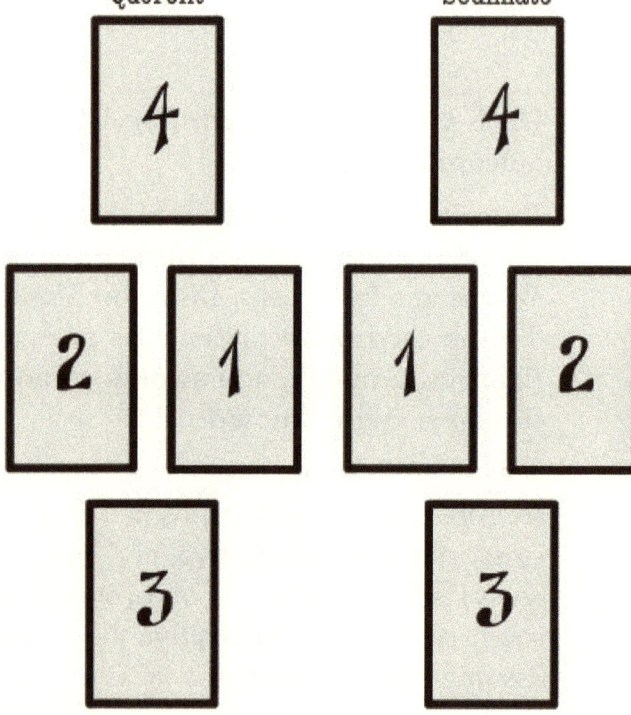

Purpose

This spread will give you insight as to where you are on your journey to finding your soulmate and vice versa.

Preparation

Cut the deck in three, moving to the left with each third. Ignore the left pile. Simultaneously draw the top cards from both piles and place them as in the diagram above.

Spread

The left set represents the querent and the right set represents their soulmate.

Interpretation

Card 1: Current life state.

Card 2: Current state of mind in regards to love.

Card 3: The lesson that has to be learned before being together.

Card 4: What will signal "now is the right time".

Specific Problem Resolution

Purpose

Use this spread if you need to figure out what steps to take in order to solve a problem.

Preparation

Shuffle as usual and spread the cards out in a fan shape. Ask a question like, "what is the best way for me to resolve the problem of...?"

Spread

There is no spread, only pull out one card at a time and read it as "this is what you must do first, this is what you must do next" until you reach a card that resolves the issue to your satisfaction. If the very first card is to your satisfaction, then the advice would be to focus on the desired outcome and your solution should be close at hand.

The Gypsy Spread

Purpose

This is a general and traditional reading that goes back to reading regular playing cards.

Preparation

Remove all trump cards from the deck. Shuffle the remaining cards and cut as usual while making a wish. Hold the whole deck facedown in your hand. Turn over one card at a time & place in a pile and say aloud, "Swords, Disks, Cups, Wands" one word per card. Each time your word matches the suit of the turned over card, move that to a pile on the right. With all the cards you've correctly named, shuffle and think of your wish again.

Spread

When ready, lay out the cards face down as indicated in the diagram. If you have more than seven cards, keep laying them out in piles, in that order, on top of the first 7. It doesn't matter if you run out of cards mid row. As you lay the cards out say aloud to each pile, "to your home, to yourself, to your love, what you do expect, what you don't expect, what is sure to come true, your wish.

Interpretation

Then turn over one pile at a time and read the cards together.

The Whole Deck Spread

1	2	3	4	5	6	7	8	9	10
11	12	13	14	15	16	17	18	19	20
21	22	23	24	25	26	27	28	29	30
31	32	33	34	35	36	37	38	39	40
41	42	43	44	45	46	47	48	49	50
51	52	53	54	55	56	57	58	59	60
61	62	63	64	65	66	67	68	69	70
	71	72	73	74	75	76	77	78	

Purpose

Use this spread when you wish to have a very detailed and lengthy reading that can easily last for an hour or more. This is a highly advanced reading and usually not done with any other reading and should probably be saved for once you are more experienced.

Preparation

Shuffle and cut as usual and then lay out all the cards, face-up, as indicated above.

Interpretation

Take your time to see stories unfold. You don't have to start at the top and read in sequence, but rather look for groupings and read together.

You may see the characters in several cards all facing the same direction, or pointing to something. You may see patterns of suits, numbers, or themes and read it as such. This is very similar to reading tealeaves, and requires a great deal of intuition.

Part V
Combination Cards with Enhanced Meaning

(Cards with similar meaning, cards of the same suit, cards with the same number, multiples, sequential numbers etc.)

Aces

When you see aces together you can assume there are lots of new starts. There is a fresh energy, renewed vitality, creativity, etc. If you have 3 aces, and other 3-cards, then look to the meaning of threes.

Twos

Twos are pairs, couples, and partners (except 2 of disks). It usually signifies teamwork and cooperation however, there are cards that hurt, wound or disrupt the twos, and they would be:

3, 5, 8, 9, 10, knight of swords

The Devil, The Hermit, The Tower, Death

Threes

The 3 of cups and the 3 of wands together is quite positive. Think group activity, celebrations, beginning a new venture etc.

The 3 of wands with 3 of swords & 3 of disks represent a very potent trial of personal fortitude.

3 of cups and the 3 of swords makes for a very emotional rollercoaster.

In general, 3s together (in fact if you have all of them including the trump card, then take this as an auspicious sign that you are being looked after by guides or angels.

Fours

The fours represent all things in the world, such as the directions, seasons, elements, and pillars, horsemen, corners of the world etc.

Having 3 4s, then you may be reminded to look into the fourth dimension or that your angels are trying to tell you something.

Fives

Fives bring about a new face, a new mask or a removal of one. They bring in the "fifth element", the pentagram, or something to throw things off balance for some reason. 3 5s would indicate holding on tight while you or your world gets thrown around for a while. 4 5s, seatbelts may be required!

Sixes

All the 6s are positive cards, but they are often placed in a balanced fashion. The thing with sixes is that they can easily get thrown off balance. A pair of 6s = good. 4 6s = great. 3 6s = off balance.

Sevens

Although the 7s on their own are not the most welcomed cards in the deck, they are also not so bad. However, seeing multiples of 7, especially if they are touching, 3 or more - then it is a very auspicious sign and should be interpreted as the difficulties that you may encounter will be like water off a duck's back.

Eights

Seeing multiple 8s means you must act quickly or the length of time depicted in the reading is very immediate or fast-paced. Multiple 4s with the 8s will cut that urgency or energy down by half. If there are more 4s than 8s, then you can expect things to go slowly. If the Chariot is also thrown in there, you can expect repeated starts and stops.

Nines

Nines signify something Divine going on even if the reading is negative in nature. It also signifies a time where you can harness Divine powers for manifesting. Having multiple 9s is like dipping your toe in the pools of other dimensions.

Tens

Multiple 10s mean that you are completing cycles in a major way. There are big influences of a mature nature involved. The 10 of swords on its own may be devastating or overwhelming but with the other 10s, especially the cups and disks, then you know things are looking up.

Pages

These are messengers, news-bearers, and communicators. The more of these you have, the more information is swirling around you, and even more so if you have trump card 11. They are also juvenile, so if you see cards like the page of cups, 6 of cups, ace of cups, 10 of disks, this can indicate a strong influence of children or preoccupation with children or large family.

Knights

The knights are like soldiers or warriors. If you see several of them, they may be men, or they may feel like aggression, or running/moving to or from things, people, or situations. They are also connected to the number 12.

Queens

Having multiple Queens show up shows a strong female influence, especially if combined with the Empress. Three Queens can also indicate, "yes" to a yes/no question.

Kings

Having multiple Kings show up shows a strong male influence, especially if combined with the Emperor. Three Kings can also indicate, "no" to a yes/no question.

Court Cards

When you see many, Pages, Knights, Queens, and Kings all in one reading, you can assume that the situation or circumstance that are occurring involve a great number of people.

Sequential Cards

If the card numbers are in sequential order, regardless of suit, then you could assume that things are progressing, moving in an upward fashion.

Cards of Love

Ace, 2, 3, 6, 10 of cups;

4 of wands, 6, 10 of disks;

The Lovers, Hierophant, The Sun

Cards of Prosperity & Achievement

Ace, 4, 6, 7, 9, 10, Queen, and King of disks;

2, 4, 6, and Page of wands;

3, 8, 9, 10 of cups;

Empress, Emperor, Hierophant, Strength, Wheel of Fortune, Sun, and World/Universe.

Cards of Patience

Ace, 2, 7, 8 of disks;

Ace, 2, 8 of swords;

Ace, 8 of cups;

Ace, 9 of wands;

Chariot, Temperance, & Universe

Cards of Friendship

3, 4, 5, page & Queen of cups;

4, Page of wands, Sun.

Positive & Happy Cards
Ace, 2, 3, 6, 9, 10 of cups;
4, 6 of wands;
Fool, Wheel of Fortune, Star, Sun, Universe.

Cards of Decisions & Choices
Ace, 4, 5 of swords;
Lovers, Justice, Hanged Man, Devil, & Judgement.

High Intensity Cards
7 of cups; ace, 5, 7, 8, 10, Knight of wands;
8 of disks; 6, Page, Knight of swords.

Cards of Sadness
5, 8 of cups; 3, 4, 8, 9, 10, Queen of swords;
Hermit, Hanged Man, Death, & Devil.

Cards of Money
Ace, 3, 4, 5, 6, 9, 10, Queen, & King of disks;
Wheel of Fortune & Emperor.

Cards Depicting Good, Honest People
Page of cups; Page, Knight, Queen, & King of disks;
King of swords; Page & King of wands;
Empress, Emperor, Hermit, Hierophant, & Hanged man.

Cards of Balance & Harmony

Ace, 2, 3, 6, 9, 10 of cups;

2, 6 of swords; 2, 6 of disks;

Empress, Emperor, Lovers, Justice, Strength, Wheel of Fortune, Temperance, & Universe

Cards of Trial

Justice, Hanged Man, & Judgement.

Notes:

Notes:

Notes:

Notes:

www.ingramcontent.com/pod-product-compliance
Lightning Source LLC
Chambersburg PA
CBHW030940090426
42737CB00007B/489